D0856539

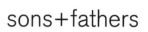

sons+fathers

First published in Great Britain in 2015
by Hutchinson

ISBN 9780091959043

This publication would not have been possible
without assistance of Park Hyatt

PARK HYATT®

sons+ fathers

Words and images supporting the Irish Hospice Foundation
Foreword by Bono / Introduction by Colm Tóibín
Edited by Kathy Gilfillan

HUTCHINSON

It is not flesh and blood,
but heart which makes us
fathers and sons.
Friedrich von Schiller

Photograph from *Instance* series
by Matthew Thompson

Contents

Foreword

It's a mysterious thing, the relationship between fathers and sons. All the bonds gathered here are different. While the stories are mainly of fathers, they are more revealing about the authors, their sons. I can't remember who said it to me but someone once did: to really know someone, you need to know their memories.

Bono

Preface

Sharon Foley
CEO, The Irish Hospice Foundation

Bono planted the seed for this book with his gift of the tender drawings he made of his father towards the end of his life, when words had ceased: in a way, the drawings were more eloquent than speech. Bono asked Kathy Gilfillan if they could be used in some manner to raise money for The Irish Hospice Foundation.

So we decided on a book and cast a net and asked others to share their own experiences of the unique bond between sons and fathers. We were thrilled by the response and generosity of the participants who are all busy, well-known people.

We believe that everyone has a right to a good death and that each one of us should expect excellent care at the end of life. Palliative care aims to achieve the best possible quality of life for people with a serious illness. It should be available for anyone with an incurable illness, regardless of age or condition. It should be available to every person, be they in a hospice, a hospital, nursing home or, of course, at home.

A key element of a good death is to have the choice of where we wish to be cared for when we die. Most Irish people prefer to die at home but many do not get that opportunity. Nursing care, provided throughout the night, can help make home deaths possible.

A share of the profits of this book will go towards The Irish Hospice Foundation's Nurses for Night Care programme. Each year, this service provides over 1400 nights of free nursing care to people with a non-malignant illness, fulfilling their final wish to remain at home at the end of their life. The demand for the service is rising and with no core state funding we rely entirely on voluntary donations to keep this vital programme going.

A percentage of the proceeds of this book will also go towards Hospice Africa Uganda founded by the inspirational Dr Anne Merriman, a Nobel Peace Prize 2014 nominee and pioneer of the hospice movement in Africa. She has introduced affordable oral morphine in Africa, utterly transforming end-of-life care for cancer patients. She says it is a human right to die free of pain and at peace. We agree.

We welcome the involvement of Park Hyatt hotels and Ardagh Group as sponsors of the book. A very special thanks to Kathy Gilfillan, Bono, Marie Donnelly, Sebastian Clayton, Colm McDonnell, Colm Tóibín, Ciarán ÓGaora, Andrew Emerson and Leo Chapman at Zero-G, Djinn von Noorden, Ed Victor, and to all the friends and contributors who, collectively, have made this book possible.

When a father gives to his son, both laugh; when a son gives to his father, both cry.

William Shakespeare

Introduction
Colm Tóibín

It is 1962 and my father is doing what I am doing now – he is at a table, writing; his head is down in concentration, his right hand is moving slowly across the page. There is chaos all around him, books piled on the floor and on the table, and notebooks open, as there is untidiness here also as I write this. I write in longhand too. We are a mirror image of each other. Sometimes when my father reads over something and doesn't like it he tears out the whole page and crumples it up and throws it towards the fireplace, often missing. I try not to do that, but I often find that my effort to be tidy has failed and there are crumpled pieces of paper around the fireplace, like old ghosts.

The image of father and son has always been complex, often dramatic. The son can conjure up the father's past just by listening about the past, by imagining what it was like. For the father, the son's future is an unknown country. Of the ways a son can enter into his father's life, Conor Cruise O'Brien has written:

> *There is for all of us a twilight zone of time, stretching back for a generation or two before we were born, which never quite belongs to the rest of history. Our elders have talked their memories into our memories until we come to possess some sense of a continuity exceeding and traversing our own individual being ... Children of small and vocal communities are likely to possess it to a high degree and, if they are imaginative, have the power of incorporating into their own lives a significant span of time before their individual births.*

It is the job of the son to live in the shadow of his father's dreams, sometimes to fulfil them, sometimes to disappoint, or indeed outshine. This makes its way into all our lives in some way or other, and also into many of the great plays of the twentieth century, works such as J.M. Synge's *The Playboy of the Western World*, where the hero claims to have killed his father, Eugene O'Neill's *Long Day's Journey into Night*, where a too-proud father is filled with vain hope for his two sons, Arthur Miller's *Death of a Salesman*, where the father and the sons can witness each other's failures, and *All My Sons*, which dramatizes a father's failure. The writer James Baldwin understood that the deep tension between the generations of men was a quintessential human story. In 1967 he wrote: 'The father-son relationship is one of the most crucial and dangerous on earth, and to pretend that it can be otherwise really amounts to an exceedingly dangerous heresy.'

It seemed important, however, for both James Baldwin and Barack Obama, as they wrote their autobiographies, to establish before anything else that their story began when their father died, to emphasize that they set out alone without a father's shadow or a father's permission. Baldwin's *Notes of a Native Son* begins with his father's death when he was almost nineteen. Barack Obama's *Dreams from My Father* begins also with the death of his father: 'A few months after my twenty-first birthday, a stranger called to give me the news,' he wrote.

Both men quickly then established their own actual distance from their father, which made their grief sharper and more lonely, but also made clear to the reader that they had a right to speak with authority, to offer this version of themselves partly because they themselves, through force of will and a steely sense of character, had invented the voice they were now using, had not been trained to be the figure they had become by any other man. 'I had not known my father very well,' Baldwin wrote. Barack Obama wrote: 'At the time of his death, my father remained a myth to me, both more and less than a man ... as a child I knew him only through the stories that my mother and grandparents told.'

For other sons, the father was deeply present and became an important and an abiding inspiration. Sometimes, nonetheless, the son learned to fulfil the father's dreams without following his example. Both Henry James and his brother William, for example, finished everything they began. This was in sharp contrast to their father, who was a great talker but did not complete much. So, too, the father of the poet W.B. Yeats and his brother the painter Jack B. Yeats, who were also great workers, good at making plans, but bad at carrying them out. It was as though the sons took what they needed from their father, his talent, and then set about offering it a completion. Their work, in all its steadfast relationship to completion, was a sort of homage to their father, but also came as a dispute with him and his indolence.

Images in literature about what the loss of a father means to a son make clear how close the bind is, or how much the father represents an anchor for a son, someone who holds the world in place. It is easy to see Hamlet as the play begins, for example, as a son made wayward by his father's death. He can be in love, and the next minute out of love, and then angry and ready for revenge and then ready to procrastinate, the next minute melancholic and the next putting on an antic disposition. Hamlet's tone can be wise and then bitter and sharply sarcastic and rude. How can he be so many things? Because his father has died not long before. That is all. He has been unmoored.

Are there any examples, on the other hand, in literature or in the lives of writers where the relationship between father and son is simple and filled with love and ease, where one generation hands on to the next with no tension, just loyalty, where memories and the experiences that gave rise to them are sweet and easy? Yes, indeed, there are such examples, and in the most unexpected places. Samuel Beckett, who was morose, wrote brilliantly about pain and loss and alienation, but none of this came from his relationship with his father, which was filled with mutual affection and ease and love. In Beckett's letters, and even in his late work *Company*, he makes clear how much he admired his father, who was a quiet-living, non-literary quantity surveyor in Dublin. Beckett relished the long walks they took together in the mountains south of Dublin. In April 1933 he wrote to a friend:

> *Lovely walk this morning with Father, who grows old with a very graceful philosophy. Comparing bees and butterflies to elephants & parrots & speaking of indentures with the leveller. Barging through hedges and over the walls with the help of my shoulder, blaspheming and stopping to rest under colour of admiring the view. I'll never have anyone like him.*

Four months later when his father died, he wrote again:

> *He was in his sixty first year, but how much younger he seemed and was. Joking and swearing at the doctors as long as he had breath. He lay in bed ... making great oaths that when he got better he would never do a stroke of work. He would drive to the top of Howth and lie in the bracken and fart ... I can't write about him. I can only walk the fields and climb the ditches after him.*

On New Year's Day 1935, in another letter, Beckett remembered a Christmas morning:

> *Not long ago standing at the back of the Scalp with Father, hearing singing coming from Glencullen Chapel. Then the white air you can see so far through, giving the outlines without the strippling. Then the pink & green sunset that I never find anywhere else and when it was quite dark a little pub to rest & drink gin in.*

These are the memories that sustained Beckett, the sort of memories that belong to us all, or those of us who have been lucky enough to have known and loved a father. They belong to me too as I put down my pen now and turn and look and see my father, oblivious to everything, having filled a new page with words, and then stopping to read over what he has written, and putting the pen towards his lips as he reads his own words, making a change here and there, the floor around the fireplace dotted with the pages we have abandoned. We turn towards each other. There is so much to say.

———

sons+fathers

Paul McCartney
+ his father Jim McCartney

When I was a kid my dad had a lot of expressions that he used and nowadays I remember them with great fondness. One of his expressions was *'Put it there if it weighs a ton.'* After he passed away I wrote a song using the essence of what he said and this is it.

Paul McCartney was born in Liverpool in 1942. Having changed the world of music forever with The Beatles, McCartney has continued to push boundaries for over forty years as a solo artist and performer, member of Wings, BRIT award-winning classical composer, half of the experimental project The Fireman, composer for the New York City Ballet with 2011's *Ocean's Kingdom* and most recently with his sixteenth studio album *NEW. The Guinness Book of World Records* lists McCartney as the Most Successful Composer and Recording Artist of All Time.

PUT IT THERE

Put it there
if it weighs a ton
That's what a father said
to his young son.
I don't care if it weighs a ton,
As long as you and I are here
Put it there
long as you and I are here
Put it there!

Paul McCartney.

Paul Auster
+ his father Samuel Auster

The news of my father's death came to me three weeks ago. It was Sunday morning, and I was in the kitchen preparing breakfast for my small son, Daniel. Upstairs my wife was still in bed, warm under the quilts, luxuriating in a few extra hours' sleep. Winter in the country: a world of silence, wood smoke, whiteness. My mind was filled with thoughts about the piece I had been writing the night before, and I was looking ahead to the afternoon when I would be able to get back to work. Then the phone rang. I knew instantly that there was trouble. No one calls at eight o'clock on a Sunday morning unless it is to give news that cannot wait. And news that cannot wait is always bad news.

I could not muster a single ennobling thought.

Even before we packed our bags and set out on the three-hour drive to New Jersey, I knew that I would have to write about my father. I had no plan, had no precise idea of what this meant. I cannot even remember making a decision about it. It was simply there, a certainty, an obligation that began to impose itself on me the moment I was given the news. I thought: my father is gone. If I do not act quickly, his entire life will vanish along with him.

Looking back on it now, even from so short a distance as three weeks, I find this a rather curious reaction. I had always imagined that death would numb me, immobilize me with grief. But now that it had happened, I did not shed any tears, I did not feel as though the world had collapsed around me. In some strange way, I was remarkably prepared to accept this death, in spite of its suddenness. What disturbed me was something else, something unrelated to death or my response to it: the realization that my father had left no traces.

He had no wife, no family that depended on him, no one whose life would be altered by his absence. A brief moment of shock, perhaps, on the part of scattered friends, sobered as much by the thought of capricious death as by the loss of their friend, followed by a short period of mourning, and then nothing. Eventually, it would be as though he had never lived at all.

Even before his death he had been absent, and long ago the people closest to him had learned to accept this absence, to treat it as the fundamental quality of his being. Now that he was gone, it would not be difficult for the world to absorb the fact that he was gone forever. The nature of his life had prepared the world for his death – had been a kind of death by anticipation – and if and when he was remembered, it would be dimly, no more than dimly.

Devoid of passion, either for a thing, a person, or an idea, incapable or unwilling to reveal himself under any circumstances, he had managed to keep himself at a distance from life, to avoid immersion in the quick of things. He ate, he went to work, he had friends, he played tennis, and yet for all that he was not there. In the deepest, most unalterable sense, he was an invisible man. Invisible to others, and most likely invisible to himself as well. If, while he was alive, I kept looking for him, kept trying to find the father who was not there, now that he is dead I still feel as though I must go on looking for him. Death has not changed anything. The only difference is that I have run out of time.

From *The Invention of Solitude* (Sun Press, 1982)

Paul Auster was born in 1947. He is the bestselling author of *Sunset Park*, *Invisible*, *The Book of Illusions* and *The New York Trilogy*, among many other works. In 2006 he was awarded the Prince of Asturias Prize for Literature. Among his other honours are the Prix Médicis Étranger for *Leviathan*, the Independent Spirit Award for the screenplay of *Smoke*, the Premio Napoli for *Sunset Park,* and the first New York City Literary Honor in fiction. He has also been a finalist for the International IMPAC Dublin Literary Award (*The Book of Illusions*), the PEN/Faulkner Award for Fiction (*The Music of Chance*), and the Edgar Award (*City of Glass*). He is a member of the American Academy of Arts and Letters, the American Academy of Arts and Sciences, and a Commandeur de l'Ordre des Arts et des Lettres. His work has been translated into forty-three languages. He lives in Brooklyn, New York.

Julian Lennon
+ his father John Lennon

And in the end, the Love you take,
is equal to the Love you make...

'The End' Lennon-McCartney

Julian Lennon was born in Liverpool in 1963, the only child of Cynthia and John Lennon. Though primarily known as a singer-songwriter, musician and producer, Julian also has a strong visual talent and has worked as a documentary film producer and a fine-art photographer. He has found a diverse base of fans for both his philanthropy and his artistic output.

Gabriel Byrne
+ his father Dan Byrne

Dreams of my Father

Last night I dreamed of you again walking in the orchard behind the house and although a thin moon hung over the fields and the stars were out I could see you as if in daylight. A shower of apple blossom rained down on you as you raised your hand in that shy half salute you always gave me, walking in the slightly hunched way that made you seem tentative, like a child entering a room of adults, your face inclined toward the window from where I watched and oh my dear, dead father, though you are always smiling in my dreams, tonight you seemed perplexed as though you wondered why you were there among the trees at that hour.

I call to you but slowly, slowly the air darkens about you and I wake with a start as if breaking from under water and all is still save the wind now, in the apple trees.

The night before, I had dreamed of the field I had not seen since a boy where the gypsies rode their wild ponies without saddles – only a piece of sacking – out over the hills, which led to the waste ground beneath the electricity pylons where I played football for Ireland and drank cider with corner boys around fires made from car tyres.

Again that extraordinary light of the moon lighting everything, even beyond the houses with the pebble-dashed walls and the forest of television aerials.

Suddenly you were there again – seeming lost as if looking for something or someone – a coat over your arm, thinner and more frail.

I ran towards you, my father, walking away from me. 'Stop!' I cried.

'I need to know where you are.'

You seemed in a hurry to be away but turned and said in a weary voice, 'You must stop searching for me. I'm not where you think I am. See, my son, over there!'

Suddenly there was a wide still river now, where the houses were, crowded with ghost people, rows deep, all those I had known and who had passed. 'It is not your time,' they are saying. 'We are happy. See how we smile. Those of us you have known and who have passed.'

And you faded and the river faded and I heard then in my dream only the whoops of wild boys urging their ponies over the gravel to the hills beyond.

Gabriel Byrne was born in Dublin in 1950 and has starred in over sixty films including *The Usual Suspects* and *Miller's Crossing*. He has written for *The Observer*, *Esquire* and *The Irish Times* amongst many others and is the author of the memoir *Pictures in My Head*.

John Pawson
+ his father Jim Pawson

Dad was a tough but kind and good man. When I think of him his Yorkshire-isms come to mind, playing in my head in a broad accent, even though he barely had one at all. A piece of advice that has stayed with me is to 'keep some brass in bank' after I spent my entire annual allowance in the first month of having a bank account. He went through the statement with me line by line, marking each entry either 'necessary', 'useful' or 'luxury'. Jingling the change in his pocket was a sure sign that he wanted to be off, the other being to wind his Movado pocket watch, which involved repeatedly sliding the case open and shut. I don't carry either change or a watch, in order to avoid mirroring the gestures, but I suspect I do unconsciously scratch my right sideburn with an upward flick of my fingers as he did, particularly since my four older sisters say I am just like him. If you asked Dad how he was, his reply most days was 'fit as a fiddle'. 'Fair to middling' was the worst it ever got, which is what he said the last time I talked to him, shortly before his death.

John Pawson was born in Halifax, England in 1949. A pioneer of architectural minimalism, he has created spare, atmospherically charged buildings all over the world and is recognized as a master of simplicity by his peers. He is married to Catherine Pawson and has two children.

Watch closed
Watch open
Pawson private collection

Sting
+ his father Ernest Matthew Sumner

A few months after my mother's funeral, it is now my father at the age of fifty-nine who will be facing his own mortality. Her death had foreshadowed and signalled his own.

He has been in and out of hospital all year. The cancer, which had begun in his prostate, has spread upward to his kidneys. Specialists, surgery, radiation and chemotherapy have all proved fruitless. He has now been committed to a hospice for the days that remain to him.

I'm led into a room there with a single bed against the wall where a crucifix hangs. I haven't seen him in a number of months and in the bed is a man I do not recognize. I imagine for a moment that they have put me in the wrong room, but the skeleton below me is my father, watching me with the bleak staring eyes of a starving child. The kind nurse who brought me in quietly pulls up a chair.

'Here's your famous son come to see you, Ernie,' she says.

'Oh aye?'

I try to compose myself; part of me wants to run out of that room like a frightened boy.

'Hello, Dad.'

'I'm going to leave you two alone now. I'm sure you have a lot to talk about,' says the nurse. Then she leaves us.

I have no idea what to say, so I take his hand in mine and gently massage the soft triangle of flesh between his thumb and his first finger. I haven't held his hand since I was small. They are big, square hands, massively knuckled with strong muscular fingers, deeply lined and grooved. My father's hands are not the delicate, expressive hands of an artist, but they have a kind of elegance, and so close to death they possess an honest and translucent beauty. They are the hands of a working man.

'Where did you come from, son?'

'I came from America last night, Dad.'

He chuckles. 'It's a long way to come to see your dad like this.'

'You were feeling better a month ago.'

He shakes his head. 'I haven't been the same since your mother died.'

I remain silent, knowing how much that small confession has cost him. I reach for his other hand and begin to massage it, but he winces. I wonder how much pain he is in. Perhaps he needs another shot of morphine. He seems a hundred years old now.

I look from his eyes to the cross on the wall and then down at his two hands cradled in mine. It is then that I receive something like the jolt of an electric shock, because apart from the colour, his hands and mine are identical. The square width of the palms, the same carved scars in the folds of the skin, the big wide knuckles wrinkled like the knees of an elephant, and the musculature fanning out from the wrists to the thick and still powerful fingers. I stare at them for a long time, turning them over and over. Why had I never noticed this before when it was so obvious?

'We have the same hands, Dad, look.' I am a child again, desperately trying to get his attention.

He looks down at the four separate slabs of flesh and bone. 'Aye, son, but you used yours better than I used mine.'

There is absolute quiet in the room. There is something like a small bird fighting to get out of my throat and I can hardly breathe. My mind is racing, trying in vain to remember when he'd ever paid me such a compliment, when he'd ever acknowledged who I was, or what I did, or what I'd achieved, or what it had cost me. He had waited until now, when his words would be devastating.

His eyes are closed now as if the last few minutes have exhausted him. It is dark outside. I kiss him softly in the centre of his forehead, and whisper that he's a good man, and that I love him.

From *Broken Music* (Simon & Schuster, 2005)

Sting was born Gordon Sumner in Wallsend, England in 1951. He is a talented musician, composer, author, activist and actor, best known as the lead singer-songwriter and bassist for rock band The Police, and for his enduring solo career. He has sold over 100 million records and is married to Trudie Styler, the film producer and actress.

Bono
+ his father Bob Hewson

'Your problem, son, is you're a baritone who thinks he's a tenor.'

With this impeccable one-liner my father, Brendan Robert Hewson, or Bob as he was universally known, nailed me.

He was great with a hammer.

Our house was, on the inside, a do-it-yourself dream. My mother was pretty good with an electric drill – practical, open-faced and a sense of humour as dark as her curls. 'Iris!' screamed my father from the top of the stairs one afternoon, having let the drill bit slip from the dowel between his knees into his groin, 'Iris! I've castrated myself!' She rushed out of the kitchen, I rushed after her, but on witnessing his DIY emasculation, she dissolved into uncontrollable laughter, to the point where she could hardly stand.

When she was gone, taken by a blood clot that turned like a switch in her head, 10 Cedarwood Road was no longer a home. It was a house of three males: my brother Norman (Nobby), me, and my grief-stricken father, who had now, to our sulking teenage eyes, become an unwanted figure of authority – a sergeant major, dishing out to my brother and me the tasks that my mother used to perform. My brother did good. I did bad. I was unaware of the hormonal drag that was going to pit me against this great man and turn me into a little bollix.

We danced until his death, the ancient ritual of son versus father. His last words were absolutely fitting. I was lying on a mattress in Beaumont Hospital beside his bed, having flown home after a U2 show in London. My father woke up in the middle of the night, anxious and whispering. His Parkinson's disease had taken some of his beautiful tenor away. The whispers were percussive, animated. I called the nurse and we both leaned in to try and make out what he was saying. Through the strained rasping, loud and clear, burst 'Fuck off!' Then, 'I want to go home. I need to go home.'

Bono is the lead singer in U2, the internationally famous band of which he was a founder member in 1976. He has been dubbed 'the face of fusion philanthropy' for successfully connecting humanitarian relief with geopolitical activism. He co-founded EDUN, the eco-fashion brand; DATA (Debt, Aids, Trade, Africa); Product Red to raise money to fight AIDS, TB and malaria and the ONE Campaign. He has helped raise money for the Irish Hospice Foundation through the drawings he made for *Peter and The Wolf* and his contribution to the *Whoseday Book* and *Art:pack*.

And he did. I'm looking forward to seeing him there. I doubt if Heaven will be as tidy as he battled for 10 Cedarwood Road to be, but this time round, that won't be my argument … God, how we loved to argue in our family. And he was the best at it.

Christmas morning was always the argument of the year. Religion. I didn't realize then that he was teaching me a great lesson: question everything. While he didn't like me to question his authority, he encouraged us to question every other authority. Here in the 1960s was a Catholic, who drove his Protestant wife and two kids to a little Church of Ireland chapel in Finglas every Sunday, attended mass in the Catholic church, then returned to pick them up. He understood that God and religion were two separate concepts, and that one could keep you away from the other. Wise is another word for his no-nonsense-Dub view of the world.

My father had spent his last few weeks conserving energy for his next adventure, largely by sleeping, where the grace of the angels, aka the nursing staff, made the incomprehensible (for any of us) as bearable as it could ever be. I had taken to drawing him as he slept; to try and stay awake, but also to meditate on what a special, talented man I had been given for a father. All my creativity comes from him. He read Shakespeare, he painted, he sang, he danced. And when he wasn't arguing with men, he made women laugh.

I have no scientific evidence to back up the claim that sometimes a close relation, in passing, bequeaths us a gift. Something to get us through. I can't explain this, but I do know that ever since my father died, my voice changed. I can sing those B's and A's with an ease I never had before. I am now a tenor pretending to be a baritone.

One Sunday morning, in an empty medieval hilltop chapel in the South of France, I knelt in an ancient wooden pew and asked my father on earth for forgiveness. I don't know if that had anything to do with it.

$\rightarrow$

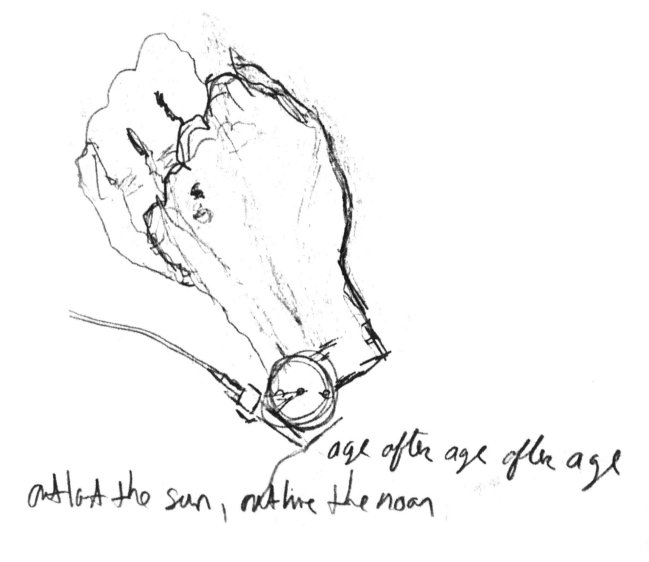

age after age after age

outlast the sun, outlive the noon

(Above) *Night Watch*, ink on paper, 2003
(Facing page) *Bob II*, ink on paper, 2003

I've hungen to you from the day of my
Birth
the day you took me from the cradle
71

(Above) **Bob III**, ink on paper, 2003

in the golden lightning
of the sunken sun
Over which clouds are brightening
that dart float and run
like an unbodied joy whose race is just begun
Shelly ode to sky lark ... drowsily off his mat
morphine — thank God for it —

(Above) **Bob asleep**, ink on paper, 2003

Rupert Everett + his father
Anthony Edward Everett

It's Christmas night 2010. For the first time since I can remember there is snow on the ground. It's a Christmas card with glitter.

'Deep and crisp and even' confirm the congregation at the midnight mass. I am standing outside the church by my father's grave, smoking. The old stained-glass window behind the altar throws a strange spangled light on the snow, and the organ and the singing sound muffled – like a memory – through the thick flint walls of the church. A lopsided moon hangs over the spire and the stars burn fiercely in the void.

The hymn ends, replaced by the friendly voice of the vicar, Colin Fox, proclaiming the good news in that comfortable Anglican brogue – caring and slightly sung, simple and familiar to villagers up and down the British Isles who still worship tradition, if not God. In the silence after the song, the natural world goes about its business. The nearby river gurgles towards the bridge. A moorhen is woken with a splash and an indignant cry. The local barn owl hoots far away on the plain.

Inside the church the congregation begin to chant the Lord's Prayer. My father is wearing his blue pyjamas and his old red slippers in the cold ground tonight. He has been dead for over a year.

From *Vanished Years* (Little, Brown, 2012)

Rupert Everett was born in 1959 in Norfolk, England. He left school at sixteen to become an actor and made his name in 1981 when he starred in the stage production of *Another Country* and later in the eponymous film version. He has appeared in over thirty films including *My Best Friend's Wedding* and has been part of many stage productions including *The Judas Kiss*. His two memoirs were published to great literary acclaim.

John Boorman
+ his father George Boorman

My father was very playful and a little pompous — rather like his son, I realize with a wince. He commanded Gurkhas in India in the First World War while his classmates were dying in the trenches in France. He played a lot of polo in India and when he finally returned to England, he found civilian life a great disappointment.

When the Second World War came along he couldn't wait to join up, but at forty he was too old for active service and they made him a clerk.

'I am typing for England,' he said bitterly.

Nothing in his life matched up to riding that horse into battle with a drawn sword, his Gurkhas charging behind him.

My mother loved him, but didn't love him enough. He was jealous of her love for me, so while he wanted me to succeed where he had failed, he also wanted me to fail. His ambition for me was clear, I would play cricket for England. He erected a net in the garden and bowled to me every day after school, hour after hour. I became a brilliant player of his innocuous off-breaks, but inept at facing better bowlers.

All my other endeavours and modest successes he swept aside; they were distractions from the primary aim. Yet when I was out for a duck or just scraped a few runs, he relished my failures as much as the pride he took in my successes. Whenever I suffered a setback in later life, his sneering smile would come to mind.

In *Hope and Glory*, the film about my childhood in the London Blitz, he was played by the great actor David Hayman, who also depicts him in my autobiographical movie, *Queen and Country*. Just as those films now seem more real to me than the memories on which they are based, so David Hayman is more like my father than my father.

In the last years of his life, he became more reconciled and we became friends. We were walking along the seafront in Brighton. He looked up at a gull perched on the sheer chalk cliff face.

'That bird is in a precarious position,' he said.

'It is a precarious position,' I replied, 'but not for a bird.'

'I know things you will never know.' He gave me that sneering smile.

We walked on in silence. I loved the way he walked. He was always striding out to the wicket from the pavilion, an imaginary bat tucked under his arm, head held high, acknowledging the applause of the crowd with a modest smile.

I am glad I did not put that scene into a film. I shall keep it to myself.

John Boorman was born in 1933. He is a film director, screenwriter and producer. Among his fifteen feature films are *Point Blank*, *Deliverance*, *Excalibur*, *Hope and Glory*, *The Emerald Forest*, *The General* and most recently *Queen and Country*. He has written and directed several radio plays. He is the author of two memoirs, *Money into Light* and *Adventures of a Suburban Boy* and co-editor of thirteen annual editions of *Projections* about the process of film making. He has seven children from two marriages. He lives in a country house in Co. Wicklow, which he bought forty-five years ago at an auction after a very good lunch.

Matthew Freud
+ his father Clement Freud

The opening page of my father's autobiography reads:

> *I was twelve years old – my prep school English master had given as homework 'write your obituary in not less than three pages'. I described my own death in some detail – painful, slow, suffered with not much courage, I wrote of Freud's impeccable prowess as a wicket keeper, and the city firm he had founded, which made him one of the richest men of his day. I mentioned the yacht and the women who were noticeable by wearing black lipstick, and finished the piece with the belief that 'his behaviour in later life meant that he will be little mourned'.*

It turned out to be less than prophetic. His death a week before his eighty-fifth birthday in 2009 was so quick as to be neither painful nor demanding of courage. He was an occasionally competent wicket-keeper but a city firm, yachts and women noticeable for any particular shade of lipstick were not in his future. Surprisingly his behaviour in later life seems to have had no effect on the great number of people mourning his passing. His fame, which irritated him during his life, produced in death such a prolific outpouring of gushing obituaries, tweets and blogs that one commentator described it as a spontaneous national round of applause.

My father was perhaps the definition of a modern polymath. Impossible to contain in one occupational category. Conventional biographies usually abbreviated to writer, broadcaster and former member of parliament, but in reality he was equally a journalist, author, performer, restaurateur, cook, gambler, horse owner, university rector, businessman, charity fundraiser, columnist, panellist and of course husband, father, grandfather and friend. Also a world-class feuder and feudee, he told me that when he took agin someone, he would usually forget but not forgive. He couldn't remember why he had fallen out with most people, but maintained the grudge regardless.

Matthew Freud was born in 1963. He is Chairman of Freud Communications, the international public relations and marketing company he founded in 1985. He is involved in a wide range of charitable, political and cultural activities, including acting as a trustee of Comic Relief and sitting on the board of the National Portrait Gallery. He is a former governor of the British Film Institute and council member of the Royal College of Art. He was also a member of the Communications Committee for the 2012 London Olympic Games.

Clement Freud with Matthew and his family on
his election to Parliament as a Liberal MP in 1973
Photo courtesy of The Guardian

And he wasn't easy to be close to. There was his unusual telephone etiquette. We had a rule that whichever one of us had hung up on the other had to make the first reconciliatory gesture: I abided by the rule, he usually didn't. His behaviour in restaurants was appalling. I had a policy of never eating anything from his plate for fear of what may have been added by a kitchen seeking revenge for his exacting and often bizarre requests or objections. There was an exhaustive and changeable list of things he couldn't 'cope' with – evidenced by a pained expression and the immediate cessation of the offending behaviour or a swift exit. The day after he died my sister Emma gave my mother a gift basket containing cigarettes, garlic, perfume and some Dr Scholl sandals, which had been on her contraband list for over fifty years.

I display many of his most deplorable character traits, although my children are less tolerant of them in me than I was with him. I also aspire to and occasionally match his best quality as one of the world's great foul-weather friends. The perfect protector in times of crisis, he went to extraordinary lengths to help or fix or commiserate and was uniquely able to find the words to lighten what seemed like unbearable burdens. I remember the countless walks of shame across Parliament Square from Westminster School to Dad's office at the House of Commons to confess my latest suspension, rustication or scrape and he always unflinchingly (and often wrongly) supported me and fought my corner. I never knew him deny a friend in need and it is a measure of the man that there was no accrued cost of his generosity. He helped with discretion, no expectation of reciprocity and no carried debt. The hardest part of losing my father was knowing that now the buck stopped with me.

Clement Freud was a working journalist for fifty-five years from 1954 when Chris Brasher commissioned a match report of a Portsmouth home game to the day he died whilst writing a column for the *Racing Post*. He became an undercover investigative journalist for *Queen* magazine, stitching up the self-important institutions of sixties London. Despite being sacked by incoming proprietor Rupert Murdoch as chief football writer of *The Sun*, he went on to become the highest-paid journalist in

→

Britain and probably the only octogenarian to have three national newspapers run his articles on one day.

I remember the frustration of visits to see Dad that were dominated by him sitting at the kitchen table next to his relentlessly manual typewriter and reading me his latest article. While I resented that he saved the best of himself for his readers, it was always obvious that he was more capable of emotion and intimacy in his writing than in any other form of expression. I am glad that my children will know him through so many millions of words left behind.

Adrian Gill said the thing he loved most about my father was that he didn't just 'not suffer fools gladly' but that he would go out of his way to find fools 'not to suffer enthusiastically' and nowhere did his appetite for confrontation find a better forum than politics. He was prouder of his fourteen years as the Member of Parliament for the Isle of Ely than any other period of his life. From his shock by-election victory in 1973 to his equally surprising ejection in 1987, he championed the rights and causes of his constituents with a dedication and diligence that shocked those who had dismissed him as a celebrity playing at politics. I recall a childhood filled with envelope stuffing, local surgeries and fête openings, letters and petitions to challenge parole hearings and protect local businesses. Using the full force of his intellect and influence, he was a constituency MP of a calibre rarely seen then and even less now.

On a national stage, Liberal politics were marginal. I think his election took the Westminster party into double figures, but he was fiercely loyal to Jeremy Thorpe in his time of great need, which was perhaps my first and formative experience of a media crucifixion up close and personal. His luck as a gambler did not desert him in parliament when he drew first place in the private members' bill ballot at odds of some 500 to one; and having briefly considered trying to legalize cannabis he put forward a freedom of information act that whilst not passed into law certainly led to the repeal of the Official Secrets Act.

He took his rejection from parliamentary service hard and having fallen out with the party bigwigs, got fobbed off with a knighthood instead of the peerage that would have given him enduring access to the Palace of Westminster that he loved. I don't think he ever drove through Parliament Square after that. I saw a lot more of him in adulthood than childhood and we found a closeness that was valuable enough to be fragile and high maintenance and endured in ebbs and flows until the end. This is the last page of his autobiography and talks about one day in 1973:

Other Freuds had been nominated for Nobel and Turner Prizes, received honorary doctorates, academic awards, freedoms of cities, companionships of honour. This Freud had been elected to parliament. 'Why aren't you looking happier?' asked Jill. Good question – it suddenly occurred to me that after nine years of fame, I now had something solid about which to be famous. I put on my happy look. It was decided to have a celebratory motorcade. I was to stand in the back of an open pick-up van with Matthew, aged nine, by my side. There were fifty cars behind us, blaring horns and flashing headlights, and we had been awarded a police escort. People waved and cheered, we waved back and Matthew said 'I think you are now the most important person in the whole world.' Deep down, just for a brief moment, I was tempted to agree with him. But remembering my role of father, I modified his opinion to 'one of the most important in the Isle of Ely'. Seeing his disappointment, I added 'which is one of the most important places in the whole world'.

We talked in later years about what the role of a father actually was. My father always thought of me as being primarily his son. I challenged him on it once, said it was hard growing up being Clement Freud's son, not really having a Christian name worth mentioning. He replied, without hesitation or apology – 'Yes, I did to you what my grandfather did to me.' I do wonder if the need to make a name for yourself isn't all the more pressing when you were raised feeling that your given name was only borrowed.

Generous as he was with everything that was in his material gift, he couldn't quite let me go, needing my achievements to be a reflection on him and my failings a validation of generational hierarchy. I loved him for all his inherited narcissism and infinitely preferred the forty-five years with him to the five I have had without. After the wrench of his death I thought I might find some freedom in not being his son anymore, but I had already lost myself completely in electing to become primarily George and Jonah and Samson's father.

———

Paul Cusack
+ his father Cyril Cusack

In the summer of 1960, following a short run in Dublin, my father took his theatre company on a European tour with *Arms and the Man* and *Krapp's Last Tape*. Each night he would play Bluntschli opposite my mother Maureen as Raina in Shaw's play. Following that, after a short interval, he would portray Krapp in Beckett's one-man play. My parents invited me to join them on the tour. I was thirteen at the time, muddling through life, shy, awkward and covered in a kind of blushing embarrassment at being in the world. Any distraction from the tedium of my adolescent preoccupations was very welcome.

The tour would take in Amsterdam, The Hague, Utrecht and Brussels. The company flew out from Dublin to Paris where they would open the tour, performing at the Théâtre des Nations festival, on the stage of the Sarah Bernhardt theatre. I went, much to my delight, in the cargo plane that carried Sean Kenny's elaborate set for the Shaw play and all the props. Things got off to a pretty disastrous start when they discovered that the set was too big for the stage and had to be re-engineered to fit. Worse still, on the morning before opening, they found that the tape recorder for Krapp, which was 'practical', had been hocked by the company stage manager to provide him with the wherewithal for drink. But it all worked out and I was full of pride sitting on my own, in a box, as my parents took their bow to rapturous applause from the Parisian audience. I was not allowed to see *Krapp's Last Tape*. My father won the International Critics Award for the best production of the festival.

It was some time during those few days in Paris that my father had a meeting with Samuel Beckett. He brought me along. I don't know why, as I had no idea who this man was or any appreciation of his significance. Someone told me, recently, that there is an account of the conversation that took place between the two men and that when Beckett asked my father what he thought of the play Cyril replied, 'I think it's a load of Protestant guilt,' to which Beckett responded, 'I think you're probably right.' I have no recollection of the conversation though I remember that my father seemed to do most of the talking. Before he left, as we stood outside the theatre, Beckett

The Cusack Family, 1951: Maureen and Cyril with Paul, Sorcha and Sinead
Photo courtesy of The Irish Examiner

→

Paul Cusack, born in 1946, is the son of Cyril Cusack. Cyril is widely considered to have been one of Ireland's finest stage and screen actors. His best-known films include *The Spy Who Came in From the Cold*, *The Day of the Jackal* and *Fahrenheit 451*. Cyril's films subsidized his work in the theatre, which was his first love. He will always be associated with the plays of Seán Ó Casey, John Millington Synge, Shaw and Chekhov. His appearance in 1990 opposite three of his daughters in *The Three Sisters* was considered a major theatrical event. Paul Cusack worked as a television producer, mainly in drama and documentaries, until he retired in 2009. He lives in Dublin with his wife Elma.

looked down at me. I think he smiled. It was a beautiful look, a look of great kindness and honesty, full of compassion for another human being. It was a connection that touched me profoundly because, in that brief moment, I realized that I wasn't alone.

The point of this story is that in the more than forty years we knew each other I never managed to have that kind of intimacy with my father. I loved him and I believe he loved me, but we were somehow unable to reveal ourselves to each other. We would meet and walk the length of Dun Laoghaire pier, talking, mostly at cross purposes, going over old painful family history that would often be followed by justifications and recriminations. Sometimes we achieved a certain closeness. One of us would tell a funny story over a pint in the Royal Marine Hotel and then we'd laugh together. But we never seemed able to look each other in the eye, man to man, so to speak, and to share, honestly, our experience of life, or to touch on our vulnerability, our humanity. And so it was that I grew to dread these meetings to the point that I chose to avoid my father altogether towards the end of his life.

In 1993, while filming in Budapest, he developed a cough and a hoarseness, which wouldn't go away. Finally it was diagnosed as motor neurone disease. He was eighty-two. I saw him, for the last time, in London, in the house in Chiswick he shared with his second wife, Mary Cunningham. A bed had been made up for him in the drawing room. There he lay, my father, the actor, speechless and motionless, attached to tubes, unable ever again to move across a stage to get a laugh or to draw a tear from a rapt audience. The only movement he could achieve now was in his right hand, and, as I sat there with him, he wrote me a note. I took it from him. 'Please promise me that I will be buried in Ireland.' When I'd read it I raised my head. He was looking at me. It was a look of almost childlike helplessness and vulnerability. I nodded, 'Of course,' and I think I smiled. A few days later he died. We brought him back to Ireland and buried him in the foothills of the Dublin Mountains overlooking the bay and the city he loved.

———

Alastair Campbell
+ his father Donald Campbell

My dad was a vet and though he never said it I think he was a bit disappointed that none of his four children went down that route. But he was a good musician too, an accomplished bagpiper and accordionist and I did inherit his love of Celtic music. Now that he has gone I am so pleased that I persevered when he was teaching me and my brother Donald to play the bagpipes as children. It led to quite a lot of piss-taking at school as we grew up in England but I always loved the pipes and I love them more than ever now. Every time I play I think of him.

One of the strongest connections I have ever felt with my dad came a couple of years ago – several years after his death – thanks to the pipes. I was asked by Sky Arts to make a film called *First Love* in which after months of training with the help of my brother Donald and a great tutor called Finlay Macdonald I played in front of two thousand people at the Royal Concert Hall in Glasgow. In between time I went to Dad's birthplace, the island of Tiree in the Hebrides, and practised with family there. At the concert I was to play a medley beginning with a tune called 'Donald Campbell', written in honour of my Dad by an old piper called George Macintyre. As I walked to the stage I caught sight of myself in a mirror and I could see my dad looking back at me, smiling. Then as I started up on stage – it was pretty nerve-wracking – I looked out and saw someone who was the complete double of my dad. I have probably never played better, before or since.

Alastair Campbell, son of a Scottish vet, was born in Yorkshire in 1957. He studied languages at Cambridge, then became a journalist, principally with the Mirror Group. His career was interrupted in the mid 1980s by a nervous breakdown, about which he has made an award-winning film. He worked as Tony Blair's spokesman and strategist from 1994 to 2003, and again during the 2005 general election. He now splits his time between writing, speaking, consultancy, charity and sport. He has written five volumes of diaries, three novels and a personal memoir on depression. A father of three children, Rory, Calum and Grace, he lives in London with his partner of thirty-four years, Fiona Millar.

Mick Heaney
+ his father Seamus Heaney

It's a melancholy exercise, remembering a loved one no longer with us. When it's a wonderful father whose strength, advice and company you could always count on, it seems an unfair one too, reducing as it does an incredibly rich life to a few selective memories. Of all the huge wrenches caused by Dad's passing, one of the strangest, not to mention saddest, is the realization that our relationship is now a one-sided affair, a monologue rather than a conversation, defined by my recollections of our time together. No matter how many shared experiences I try to recall, I know that they can never begin to tell the story of our time together. The best I can hope for is a blurred snapshot, and a highly subjective one at that. (By way of underlining this point, anyone looking for insight into the literary imagination of Seamus Heaney may as well turn the page now.)

But just as we have treasured family photos, so there are moments encapsulating different stages of our family's life to which I find myself returning again and again. There was the excitement that greeted Dad's return to our home in Wicklow after what seemed like an interminable absence abroad – in reality, six weeks in Berkeley during the spring of 1976 – though, truth be told, much of my joy probably pivoted around the swag of impossibly exotic American toys he brought back for us, chief among them a die-cast model airplane in bright yellow, red and blue. But still, never having been separated from him so long, I can still feel the air of expectation in the days before his homecoming, as well as the elation and sense of completeness when he was finally back with Mum, Chris, Catherine and myself.

A decade or so later, it was me crossing the Atlantic to be reunited with the family, this time for Christmas in America, where Dad was teaching at Harvard for a year. One morning, as the pair of us strolled through Cambridge streets damp with melting snow, Dad splashed his way through a sidewalk puddle, mainly to show off the Doc Marten boots that he, like me, was wearing. 'Doc conquers all,' he said, grinning away. That such an ostensibly throwaway remark should thrum with understated emotion, even at the time, is no accident: it was Dad's expertly weighted way of voicing affection without indulging in anything so embarrassing to his twenty-one-year-old son (and maybe even to himself) as a declaration of paternal love.

Of course, just in case it appears that all our dealings were suffused with a rose-tinted glow, there was a fair bit of cut and thrust too, particularly during my adolescence. There was, for instance, the morning when Dad supposedly did me a favour by giving me a lift to school. Instead, the short journey was accompanied by a catalogue of standard parental gripes – scruffiness of uniform, dog-eared nature of school books, etc. – so relentlessly grumpy as to be unintentionally hilarious. That the incident became something of a family joke says much about his powers of stern discipline.

But for whatever reason, I keep harking back to the afternoon Chris and myself passed with Dad in a London pub in January 2013. He had given a typically marvellous reading at the Irish embassy the previous evening, and as Mum and Catherine went about their own business that morning, me and my brother received a text from Dad wondering if we fancied a swift pint before we took the plane back to be with our own families in Dublin. It was barely midday, but the prospect of an ever-so-slightly cheeky drink was irresistible.

We spent an hour at the most in the pub he suggested, a Soho watering hole once frequented by the London literati. We didn't talk about anything especially important – beyond a running gag about whether it was 'too early for a brandy' I don't remember anything we said – but amidst our mild giddiness there was the unstated yet palpable sense that such moments were to be cherished, as they were a finite resource.

Just how finite we did not then know, thankfully. One of things I miss most about Dad is having those kinds of conversations, where nothing of consequence was said because there was no need to, and I could just bask in his company. So to remember these moments can be heartbreaking. But it's a pleasure too.

Mick Heaney was born in Belfast in 1966. The eldest son of the late poet Seamus Heaney and his wife Marie, he grew up in Wicklow, Dublin and Boston with his brother and sister. A journalist and broadcaster, he is currently radio columnist for the *Irish Times* as well as a regular television contributor on the arts. He lives in Dublin with Emer and their two daughters.

Dylan Jones
+ his father Michael Jones

When I was young, my father and I always fought. Actually, that's not strictly true, as it was my father who fought, my father who hit me, my father who would hit me so much that I would cower whenever he entered the room. He hit me so much that at the age of ten I stammered so much that I found it impossible to say my own name.

So when I left home at the age of sixteen I was sort of leaving for good. After one final confrontation with my father, I decided I wanted out. We stayed in touch, he would occasionally help me financially, and I often went home for Christmas, but ours was a troubled relationship. It got better – obviously, it had to get better – and we learned to spend time together without ever acknowledging the past, but those early years stayed with both of us in ways that we never bothered to articulate. At least not to each other.

After a while, our relationship seemed to become like the relationships that many fathers have with their sons: he would berate me for not achieving what he thought I was capable of, often referring to what I did as 'rubbish'. Yet I could tell that he was secretly proud of me; he just couldn't find a way to tell me.

One of the accidental by-products of ageing is finding out what clichés are true. And so regardless of what decisions you make along the way – monumental or seemingly incidental – a lot of life is determined for you. This was the case I suppose with our relationship: after a while it was always going to be this way.

When my father died, my brother and I went to empty his flat. His death had left me strangely unaffected, although spending a day dismantling what was left of his life was the hardest thing. The day was not without its comic moments, as my brother and I divided his belongings like a couple embarking on a divorce ('No, it's OK, you can have the wagon-wheel coffee table. The Phil Collins CD? Actually you can have that too if you like…'). The process was as much a bonding exercise as a cathartic one.

But it was the briefcases under the stairs that threw me. My father had always been a keen collector of my work, and whenever a photograph of me appeared in a newspaper, or whenever I'd written something for a magazine – no matter how small – he had found it, cut it out, and regularly pasted it into a scrapbook, had it mounted on cardboard, or even, sometimes, framed. He had honoured my brother in a similar way, covering the walls of his bedroom with photographs of Dan getting another promotion or military medal, but you can write a lot of columns in thirty years, and my father had seemingly collected all of them. I'm no slouch when it comes to archiving my own work, yet my father had found and kept articles, features and reviews that I'd long since forgotten.

His bookcases were full of my books – sometimes three or four copies of the same one – including a couple I'd written or contributed to early in my career, which I was so embarrassed about I didn't even have them myself.

Just when I thought I'd found everything of mine he had collected, I discovered four metal briefcases that were full of cuttings from a newspaper I had worked on back in the nineties. There they were, all my cuttings, carefully glued into A4 booklets, each one with the date of its appearance scribbled in dark-blue ink in my father's own spidery writing.

All I could do was stare. His obsession didn't border on anything other than love. Ever since I had started to appear in print, he had collected me. Collected my life. A life he had helped build. Maybe he had collected them because he thought that one day they would run out, that one day there wouldn't be anything else to collect. But there it all was, scraps of a life told though scraps of a talent.

My brother didn't need to ask which one of us was going to keep these, and, in an act of something more than brotherly love, he just started carrying them out to my car. I've still got the boxes at home, pushed under the stairs in my house. I never look at them, but then I don't need to.

My father did that for me.

Love you, Dad.

Dylan Jones was born in 1960 and educated at Central Saint Martins in London. He is a prolific writer and journalist who has edited *GQ* magazine in the UK since 1999. He was awarded the OBE in 2013 for services to publishing and the fashion industry. He is married with two children.

Mario Testino
+ his father Mario Testino Snr

I was probably not the sort of son my father expected but this never stopped him from being the most generous with me. He gave me a lot of freedom and at the end was almost the one that pushed me forward into being me.

The best advice he gave me was in life there is what you want and what life wants. Life is more powerful than you so pay attention.

Everything that I became seemed to have been chosen by life, not necessarily by me!

Mario Testino was born in 1954 in Lima, Peru, the eldest son of an Italian businessman and an Irish mother. He came to London in 1976, took a flat in an abandoned hospital and began selling portfolios to beginner models. He is now at the top of his profession and is best known for his highly polished, exquisitely styled fashion spreads and advertising campaigns. The late Diana, Princess of Wales, chose him for her famous *Vanity Fair* cover in 1997. His work is now in major museums and galleries but he carries his fame lightly and has quietly worked for Peruvian and international charities.

Mario Testino and his father
Testino private collection

Max McGuinness
+ his father Paul McGuinness

McGuinneysses

Stately, plump Paul McGuinness came from the stairhead, bearing a bowl of lather on which a mirror and a razor lay crossed. Although in actual fact there was no razor at all because some ungrateful progeny had swiped his stubble-slicer and not bothered to return it. Shite and onions! he bellowed whilst seeking another means of paring his visage, before happening upon the very same foam-flecked shaver lodged surreptitiously in the adjacent bathroom.

The ablutions done, Paul stood up and went over to the parapet whence he surveyed the proceeds of rock and roll – mares in foal, a well-sprung hare gambolling across the grassy knoll, and, the rhododendrons, at last, blissfully under control. All seemed to be progressing well, till he glimpsed an aesthetic outrage, which made him want to yell: the corner of the greenhouse beyond the trees could still be seen! Such an unforgivable intrusion upon the pastoral scene!

Still cursing the rudeness of the angle, he proceeded to take a dunk in a pool which, quite unlike the 40-foot at Sandycove, was neither snotgreen nor in the least scrotumtightening – a balmy breaststroke hither and thither and then … launching himself with relish upon the inner organs of beasts and fowl. Putting a forkful into his mouth, chewing with discernment the toothsome pliant meat, he pondered the future of the recording industry, plotted revenge against a recalcitrant ISP, then resumed consuming the rest of the succulent kidney.

Though seeing as I've been willfully violating the intellectual property rights of the Joyce estate for the past few minutes, perhaps we should call it evens.

By lorries along Sir John Rogerson's Quay Mr McGuinness walked soberly, past Windmill Lane, Leask's the linseed crusher's, the sailors' home, Principle Management, the postal telegraph, a loop the loop around the Green, past the old

Max McGuinness was born in Dublin in 1986. He attended Oxford and is currently completing a Ph.D. in French literature at Columbia. His writing has appeared in a variety of Irish and international publications including *The Dubliner*, *The Stinging Fly* and *The White Review*.

$\rightarrow$

Max, Paul and Alexandra McGuinness at U2
Oakland Coliseum, 7 November 1992
Photo courtesy of B.P. Fallon

Dandelion Market where an eon or two before, he first clapped eyes on Bono Boylan and the lads. Ah yes jingle jaunty Blazes Bono. Stepping in dark shoes and socks with skyblue clocks to the refrain of 'I Will Follow'. In the audience a slut shouts out of her: eh mister Bono! Your fly is open, mister Bono! But McGuinness, hovering discreetly at the back, has taken their measure. Having concluded their set, the teenage musicians trepidatiously approach the man browsing the newspaper with Olympian indifference. And without even looking up from his copy of the *Freeman's Journal*, he says: you don't really know how to play your instruments, do you? A pause. And then: but, Blazes Bono, Bono Boylan or whatever you're called, tell me this: would you be interested in breaking America? Because I am.

He entered Davy Byrne's. Moral Pub. He doesn't chat. Hell he probably hasn't even been there in over twenty years but I've started so I'll go on. Now they don't serve gnudi or crudo or lamb hamburgers or what have you in Davy Byrne's Moral Pub. So McGuinness orders a glass of burgundy and a gorgonzola sandwich. And frankly, they don't serve that in Davy Byrne's either, but they did once upon a time, so bear with me. An acquaintance accosts him – I would transform the character into someone here but it's not very flattering so I'll leave it as it is:

> *Blazes Bono and the lads well? asked Nosey Flynn.*
> *Quite well, thanks, McGuinness replied … a cheese sandwich, then. Gorgonzola, have you?*
> *Doing any singing these times, Blazes Bono?*
> *Music. Knows as much about it as my coachman.*
> *Mustard, sir?*
> *Thank you.*

And so, hastening through a few hundred pages, we leave him to the cheese sandwich in the snug embrace of Davy Byrne's on Bloomsday 16th June, the day of Ulysses and the birthday of my father, Paul.

———

Cillian Murphy
+ his father Brendan Murphy

My father and I on my first
trip to the Blasket Islands, 1979
Murphy private collection

Cillian Murphy was born in County Cork, Ireland in 1976, the oldest child of a family of educators. He was drawn to performance after encountering the Corcadorca Theatre Company. Cillian began his show-business career as a rock musician but devoted himself to acting when he made his debut in Enda Walsh's *Disco Pigs*. In 2002 his career went from independent productions to mainstream with his role in Danny Boyle's *28 Days Later*. Neil Jordan cast him as 'Kitten' Brady in *Breakfast on Pluto* and he has proven himself to be charismatic and protean on screen and in theatre with over forty film roles including the *Batman* films. He is married to Yvonne McGuinness with whom he has two children.

Joseph O'Connor
+ his son James O'Connor

First School Disco

Yesterday, at his birth, I could hold him in
  one hand.
Fervent, his stare at the monochrome new.
On the nights he didn't sleep, I knelt by
  his crib,
Lulling lines from old songs I didn't know
I remembered.

A night owl, curious, enthralled by blue
  shadows,
Chuckling at angels
He glimpsed in the curtains.
The embers of a fireplace,
Towards which he stretched
  his hands,
As he rolled on the rug after bath-time.

Ireland was changing.
We brought him home from London,
Through the wintry land of England.
Christmas when we came.
Drinkers on the ferry
Singing 'Fairytale of New York'
As the lights of Dun Laoghaire,
My boyhood town,
Appeared in the beer-steamed windows.

I blinked. Eleven years
Went past in a lullaby.
My son beside me now
As we drive through the dusk,
Reads names from redundant posters
Of presidential candidates,
As they dampen on the passing lampposts.

Joseph O'Connor was born in 1963 and is the author of eight novels: *Cowboys and Indians*, *Desperadoes*, *The Salesman*, *Inishowen*, *Star of the Sea*, *Redemption Falls*, *Ghost Light* and *The Thrill of it All* and two collections of short stories, *True Believers* and *Where Have You Been?*. He has also written radio diaries, film scripts and stage plays. Among his awards are France's Prix Millepages, Italy's Premio Acerbi, the *Irish Post* Award for Fiction, the Nielsen BookScan Golden Book Award, an American Library Association Award, the Hennessy/*Sunday Tribune* Hall of Fame Award, the Prix Littéraire Européen Madeleine Zepter for European Novel of the Year and the Irish PEN Award for Outstanding Achievement in Literature. He is the Frank McCourt Professor of Creative Writing at the University of Limerick.

Quiet in the car.
Wipers moving rain.
The names he utters gently
Like a necklace he's assembling
From beads he once found in an old
    box of toys.

At the school, he combs his hair,
Checks his Man United shirt,
Greets his teachers with a nod,
Looks nervous, excited.
'Dad, will you stay?
You can, if you want.
It's only six to seven.
We'll be finished in an hour.'
Maybe better to leave.
The truth is, I can't.

Here come the glittered girls. And here the
    hearty boys,
Pucking one another as the disco begins,
On the night of my firstborn child's first dance.
Jedward doing 'Fight For Your Right To Party'.
Lady Gaga's manifesto: 'Want Your
    Bad Romance'.

I'd always thought I wouldn't mind,
Would wear his growing lightly,
Shrugging off the milestones,
Consoling his mother.
But it's me who feels the ache
In the shadows of my joy,
Flicker-lit by strobe and by knowing
    where we are.
Wishing I could hold him, one last time.
Or wishing I could join him
On air guitar.

———

Michael Craig-Martin
+ his father Paul Craig-Martin

In the mid 1990s I was visiting my father Paul, who was eighty-seven and in a nursing home in Dublin. I took him out to lunch. He was nearly blind, quite deaf, and very frail, just able to walk, but in other ways surprisingly well and alert. As usual, he had a gin and tonic followed by three full courses with wine.

As we were having coffee he said, 'You know the way I used to like doing woodworking, making shelves and bits of furniture? Well I've started again.' Startled by the news, I asked how he was managing this. 'I do it all in my head,' he explained. 'I draw up the plans, cut the wood, knock in the nails, everything, right down to cutting my finger.'

He smiled. 'Do you know what the last thing I made was? A special saw I needed for making the other things – and it works!'

Michael Craig-Martin RA was born in 1941 in Dublin. He grew up in the United States and was educated at Yale. He is a conceptual artist and painter, well known for his vividly coloured images of ordinary objects. He is a key figure in the art world and his work is in many public collections including the Museum of Modern Art, New York, the Tate Gallery, London, and the Centre Georges Pompidou, Paris. He taught for many years at Goldsmiths College, University of London, where he was an influential teacher to his students. He lives and works in London.

Artwork by Michael Craig-Martin

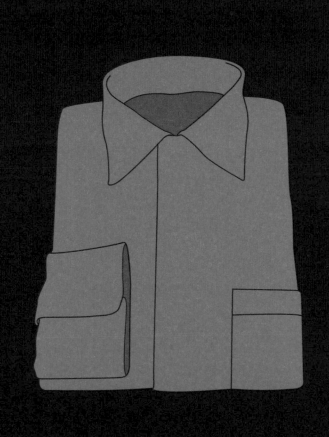

Paul McGuinness
+ his father Philip McGuinness

My father, Philip Patrick McGuinness, was the youngest of twelve children of a clerk in the Mersey Docks & Harbour Board. He was born in 1922 and died in 1980 from a heart attack. He went to a Catholic high school in Liverpool, where he excelled at maths, English and football.

By November 1941 he was in the RAF and on a troopship bound for South Africa where flying training was conducted. He was twenty years old when his occasionally kept diary records that he was in Gwelo, southern Rhodesia. He seems to have enjoyed his time in Africa and there are souvenirs amongst his papers that demonstrate a lively colonial social environment. The British plan to win the war by attacking Germany from the air had led to the formation of Bomber Command and training the crews took place in different parts of the Empire.

On 21 December 1943 he was flying the first of his fifty-seven operations over Germany and other parts of occupied Europe. That first mission was to bomb Frankfurt at night, flying in a Halifax. The return flight took five hours and forty minutes according to his neatly handwritten logbook. He was a navigator in 35 Squadron, part of the elite Pathfinder Force that went first and was supposed to mark the target for the main force of many hundreds of bombers by setting it on fire with incendiaries and flares.

I wish I had asked him more about his wartime experiences; in retrospect I know he was reluctant to discuss them. He survived the war but more than 55,000 Bomber Command aircrew were killed. I now know that he must regularly have had the appalling experience of seeing their empty beds as his friends failed to return.

What it was like for a kid of twenty-one to fly off in a Lancaster bomber with primitive navigational equipment, responsible for his crew's lives, responsible for finding their destination, being shot at by enemy aircraft, dodging flak, seeing other planes hit and

Paul McGuinness was born in 1951 in Germany. His parents were an RAF officer, Philip McGuinness, and a schoolteacher, Sheila Lyne. He grew up around the world on various military bases. He went to boarding school in Ireland then Trinity College Dublin from where he did not graduate. He worked as an assistant director in film for a few years before meeting U2 in 1978 when they were seventeen and he was twenty-seven. He managed them until 2013 when he and Trevor Bowen sold their company, Principle Management, to the band. He was one of the founding partners of TV3 Ireland and is one of the owners of Ardmore Film Studios. With composer Bill Whelan he is a partner in McGuinness Whelan Music, the publishers of *Riverdance*. He is married with two children.

destroyed, is unimaginable. He must have been terrified. I'm sure he was affected by it for the rest of his life.

He was commissioned, decorated, and stayed in the RAF as a career officer after the war. He met my mother in Cork whilst on leave in 1947. They married in Liverpool in 1949 and I was born in a British army hospital, formerly SS, in Rinteln, near Hanover, in 1951. He had been posted there as part of the post-war occupation of Germany. The British zone was in the north. By now, based at RAF Bückeburg, his flying activity was transporting Allied officials around the world. From his logbook I know that on the day I was born, on 16 June 1951, he flew as navigator in an Anson no. PH 725 from Bückeburg to Gutersloh and back. A Wing Commander Taylor was the pilot.

He was posted to a new RAF base every couple of years so I grew up in RAF Thorney Island, RAF Cosford, Malta, Poole and Aden. In each place I went to a new school and had to make new friends. Though I was always being told that I was Irish by my parents, I had never been to Ireland until 1962, when, at the age of eleven, I was sent to Clongowes Wood College, a Jesuit boarding school in County Kildare.

My father brought me over himself on the B&I Line mail boat from Liverpool to Dublin. Passing through his hometown I met some of his family. I have not had much contact with any of them since. Being the youngest sibling, they mostly died before him.

I remember the trip vividly. He hired a car in Dublin and delivered me and my trunk and tuck box to Clongowes and after the handover he drove away. I kissed him goodbye halfway down the long avenue and walked back to the school. For the next few days, never having been so devastated by loneliness before, I would visit the place where his tyres had flattened the grass.

I spent six years at Clongowes. After a shaky start, I got the hang of it. At first I couldn't understand the accents, and I thought Ireland was primitive compared to England. I made some good friends, some of whom I still have at the age of sixty-three. There were boys at the school whose families had more money than mine. I resented that. I started to get holiday jobs when I was home from school. I worked as a waiter, dishwasher - menial jobs. During those teenage years my relationship with my father deteriorated. I didn't work hard at school. My father couldn't understand why I wasn't making the most of this wonderful opportunity to get an education and proceed through

→

university to a proper career as a doctor or lawyer. I did the minimum to get by and eventually scraped into Trinity College Dublin to study philosophy and psychology where again I did the minimum, preferring girls, music, student theatre and journalism. I was always broke despite having a full grant from Dorset Education Authority. My parents were thoroughly disappointed and thought I was blowing it. Things got pretty tense at home and when I failed to attend the required number of lectures and was therefore not allowed to sit my third year exams, I came home to Poole, where my parents were living, with my tail between my legs. My father had by now retired from the RAF and had picked up some qualifications that enabled him to become a teacher like my mother. He was teaching maths and statistics in Bournemouth College.

Having lost my grant, I couldn't afford to return to Trinity and repeat the year. The only thing I could afford was to enroll at the University of Southampton and live at home, commuting by train. I hated it and hated my parents for not having the money to send me back to Dublin, where my girlfriend and all my other friends lived. My relations with my father got to the point where we were hardly speaking. I was very condescending and he was angry. I thought I was much more sophisticated than he was. He regarded the things that I had been doing at Trinity, theatre, magazines etc. as frivolous. I'm sure I was fairly obnoxious. He thought I was wasting my life.

One day I didn't get off the train at Southampton and carried on to London where I spent a dissolute year. I managed to save some money before returning to Trinity to repeat my third year.

By the time I got back to Trinity many of my friends had moved on and I was bored with philosophy. I got a job on a movie and dropped out once and for all. After that first movie I continued to work in films and TV commercials as a freelance assistant director. My parents did not regard this as a proper career. When I would go home to Poole for Christmas the mood was gloomy. I promised that I would eventually go back to Trinity and finish the degree but I didn't really mean it.

By this time I had discovered the music business. At the same time as managing a couple of small music acts, I continued to work in film. I was becoming ambitious and developing a feel for show business. I look back on that period

Squadron Leader Philip Patrick McGuinness
McGuinness private collection

with some pleasure. I had a car and a loving loyal girlfriend. I had met U2 in 1978 and had started working with them to try and obtain a record deal.

My parents were now living in Dublin. My brother lived in Ireland too and my sister Katy was at school in Killiney and was a much better student than I had ever been and was about to go to Trinity and become a lawyer. My father was enjoying his life. Kathy and I got married. My father loved Kathy very much and I think may have been a little puzzled as to what she saw in me. Our wedding in Trinity Chapel and the Shelbourne Hotel was cool. My father and I were getting on better and he came to the concert in the National Stadium on 26 February 1980, which turned out to be the night U2 were spotted by Island Records to whom they subsequently signed. I think he could sense there was something significant happening. He came round to my flat a month or so later and we had a proper talk about what a record deal was and how the music business worked. For the first time I had the feeling that he was impressed and proud of me. That was the last time I saw him alive.

Shortly after that U2 were in Windmill Lane Studios in Dublin recording their first album. Kathy and I had gone to New York, me for the first time ever. The reason for my trip was to try and meet the great agent Frank Barsalona, who I wanted to book the band's live appearances. He hadn't given me an appointment when I phoned the first time.

Then I got a call from my mother in Dublin to say that my father had died suddenly. I phoned Barsalona to say my father had died and I wouldn't be able to see him for a week or so. He HAD to give me an appointment. That was the beginning...

In the years after 1980 and until 2000, when she died, my mother enjoyed enormously the success that the band and I had. She lived to see our wonderful children Alexandra and Max thriving as teenagers. She read everything about me,

→

followed the ups and downs, witnessed me do other things like TV3 and Ardmore Studios. She came on U2 tours, saw great places on holiday with my family and me. I wish my father had seen these things too. He would have loved it. Had he lived longer, I would have enjoyed asking for his advice. It took me a long time to realize how much I loved and admired him. We wasted a lot of time on competition when we should have been kinder to one another. I remember in my teens I would challenge him on topics like nuclear disarmament. I was starting to enjoy the cut and thrust of argument as sport. That must have been so hurtful for him.

Even by the end of WWII the effectiveness and the morality of area bombing had become a subject of dispute. Some took the view that the crews of Bomber Command were war criminals. Most sensible people took the view that they were heroes. That debate continues.

Amazingly the animals that had died for the Empire got their memorial before men like my father. The memorial to military horses, camels, dogs and carrier pigeons killed alongside British forces was inaugurated in 2004 and is on Park Lane opposite the Dorchester.

It was not until 2012 that the Bomber Command Memorial near Hyde Park Corner was finally erected and unveiled by the Queen. Kathy and I and my sister and her husband were invited to this moving occasion, which came at the end of a long and sometimes bitter campaign to commemorate the 55,573 men who had died.

Every time I pass it, I think of my father.

———

Peter Sís
+ his father Vladimír Sís

Illustration by Peter Sís

Peter Sís was born in Brno, Czechoslovakia, in 1949. He trained at the Academy of Applied Arts in Prague and the Royal College of Art in London. He began his film career and won the Golden Bear Award in 1980 at the Berlin Film Festival, the Grand Prix Toronto and the Cine Golden Eagle Award. In 1982 the Czech government sent him to Los Angeles to produce a film for the 1984 Winter Olympics. When the Eastern Bloc boycotted the Olympics, Peter was granted asylum in the United States and stayed to carve out a highly successful career as an illustrator and author, with more than twenty books and as many awards to his name. In 2014 he completed the tapestry in honour of Seamus Heaney that hangs in Dublin Airport. Peter lives in the New York City area with his wife and children.

Jonathan Wells
+ his father Arnold Wells

— I —

For my father the Cadillac Fleetwood Brougham that took him in and out of New York City each day offered more than physical transportation. The back seat was his sanctuary where he could spend an uninterrupted hour alone. He paged through the *New York Times* and thumbed the stacks of business papers that he brought home each night. Mostly, they stayed undisturbed inside his briefcase as he stared out the window and listened to Bach's unaccompanied cello partitas, his favourite music.

Being alone with him in his car travelling into what I considered 'his city' was as great a privilege as it was a rare one. Attilio, his giant Neapolitan driver, steered the car along the route my father had selected, his mournful clown's face with spiky black hair reflected to the back seat in the rear-view mirror. Dad was very precise in his driving instructions to Attilio. 'Always pump the brakes. Never stomp on them. Remember, they are as sensitive as we are,' he said. 'Anticipate the turns, don't yank the wheel,' he repeated often, for my sake as well as Attilio's.

When we were alone my father didn't harp on about my lack of weight or not eating enough. He saved those jibes for a bigger audience. The car was his classroom for the one-on-one tutorial, his pulpit, and he was uncharacteristically serious. There, he handed down his experience of the world as he understood it and as he expected me to learn it.

Even though I had become an avid reader he thought it was time to teach me how to read as he had taught himself to. Cocking his head slightly to the side, he said, 'I've been watching you and I think you're taking too long on each page. Are you looking at every word?' he asked. I looked at him, surprised that reading could have more than one strategy. 'Is that wrong?' I asked. 'Well, not wrong exactly, but who has time for the little words? Do you really need 'the' and 'and' and 'if' or helper

Jonathan Wells was born in 1954. His poems have appeared in *The New Yorker, Ploughshares, AGNI* and the Academy of American Poets *Poem-A-Day* programme among other reviews and journals. His first collection, *Train Dance*, was published by Four Way Books in 2011 and his second collection, *The Man With Many Pens*, will be published by Four Way Books in autumn 2015. He edited an anthology of poems about rock and roll titled *Third Rail*, which was published by MTV Books/Pocket Books in 2007.

verbs? Those won't give you the gist of it. They can be skipped and you won't be missing much.' He examined me to make sure I was following him closely. 'No articles, prepositions or pronouns is my motto. They just get in the way and confuse the sentence. You need to get to the meat as quickly as possible. Don't waste time on vegetables. If you take all of those bitty words out, you'll reach the same conclusion. I call it vertical reading. Horizontal is for scholars. You don't want to be one of them, do you?' he asked, baiting me to say yes.

He thought for a moment, pleased with how well he had explained the lesson. Then he asked, 'Do you have a girlfriend yet?' I looked at him, not sure what the right answer was. 'Well, I go to dancing school if that's what you mean,' I answered. 'No, I know you go to dancing school. What I meant was of the girls you dance with, is one of them special?' He looked at me carefully. The tic where he scrunched up his right eye and lifted his cheek was particularly pronounced. 'No, not really. I don't have a favourite if that's what you mean. I don't really care who I dance with except for some of the tall girls. I avoid them.' 'By the time I was thirteen, I had already had many girlfriends but I lived in a city and there were lots of girls to play with. What kind of girl do you like?' he asked with genuine interest. 'I don't know yet, Dad,' I said. 'Well, you should start to think about it. You have no idea how exciting life can be with them,' he said and looked at me cryptically as if he were speaking in code. 'I can't imagine why they'd want to talk to me.' 'Nonsense,' he said. 'They want you to talk to them, to transport them somewhere. Anywhere you'd like to go. Do you know what I mean?' he asked. 'No,' I said. 'Well, you need to feed their imagination with a place they've never seen before, an unknown place. Describe it to them and take them there with your words. Help them imagine it. Doesn't matter whether you've been there or not. They haven't been there either.'

When he said this I remembered the standard question he asked young women we met on our vacations. 'Are you from Tacoma by any chance?' he'd ask. My brother Tim and I thought he had some geographical sixth sense of knowing where a woman was from until we realized that he asked all of them the same question. He thought it was unlikely that anyone we met in the northeast was actually from Tacoma or knew anything about it. Once he was certain, he would begin to describe what a beautiful place it was, how the sailboats looked in the light in Commencement Bay, the arrangement of the islands in the distance and the faint smell of cherry blossoms in the spring.

$\rightarrow$

Jonathan Wells and his father Arnold Wells
Wells private collection

My father opened the door to his room at the Hotel Georges V in Paris appearing as fresh as if he had just awakened from a full night's sleep rather than having flown that morning from New York. His black hair glistened. His clothes were uncreased. He gave me a hug and said he'd be back in a minute. I sank into the overstuffed sofa and hoisted the cast that protected the leg I had broken two months before onto the marble coffee table. It was a relief to be away from my plain boarding-school room in Lausanne for a few days.

When he was finished he looked at my cast and came over to give it a knock with his knuckle. 'Holding up I see. Still solid. How are your shoulders doing?' he asked. 'Have the crutches helped build up your muscles? Let me see … flex…' he commanded. I looked at him to ask if I really had to and the answer in his brown eyes was clear. 'Not bad … not bad. Could be a lot better. Look, I'm busy during the days but we can have dinner together every night. Here's some money. Get what you want. If you run out I'll give you more.'

During the days I walked the streets for as long as I could stand on my crutches. I went to art museums and bought a green crushed velvet suit and stack-heeled green suede boots. Whatever I wanted Dad let me have, the value of money lost on both of us.

My meals alone with him were a mixture of reminiscence and exhortation. He repeated the stories he'd told me before about the Depression and how his father had been out of work for ten years, most of which he had spent playing pinochle. 'That's why,' he added, 'it is so important for you to build your body. I want you to be a man of substance, not air, not a *Luftmensch* like my father's friends were. They never went back to work. They got thinner and thinner. In the old days the *Luftmenschen* floated from town to town. They told stories. They had no gainful employment. No regular meals. Do you want to be one of those? That's why I insist that you eat and do the strength exercises I designed for you.'

On the Saturday afternoon before I was scheduled to return to school he announced that he wouldn't be able to have dinner with me but we could have a drink together instead. When the time came I put on my new green suit, the right pant leg ripped to the thigh to accommodate the cast, my new paisley shirt and one boot. Riding down in the elevator with its crossed gilded arrows and laurel leaves I looked in the mirror and felt confidence.

Dad ordered a vodka and tonic and a Coke for me. 'I'm sorry I can't stay with you tonight and I want to make it up to you. Would you like company?' At first I didn't understand what he meant. I had a friend who lived in Paris but I hadn't called him. 'Cyril isn't here,' I said. He turned sideways to look at the three women who were

→

sitting at the bar. 'That wasn't what I meant. I meant one of them,' he said. 'Which one do you like?' he asked as if he had already chosen. He tapped the brass room key on the glass-topped table. The trio turned around in unison and stared at him. 'Which one do you want or should I pick for you?' he asked.

After they had swivelled their brittle hairdos toward us to see who had summoned them I fixed on the dark-haired girl on the right. The kohl liner around her eyes and her olive skin felt like the challenge of the unknown or the inarticulate or both. She looked like Claudia Cardinale, curvy and ample. Dad gestured to her theatrically and she walked over to us and pointed at me to make it clear he was only the financier. He said, 'Show her your room key so she can see the number.' She nodded as if no other explanation were needed. Pointing at his watch and holding up all ten fingers, he gestured at the cast as if to say that that was how long it would take me to get to the room. It didn't cross my mind to refuse her or him.

Dad nudged my elbow as if to set me in motion. I moved slowly along the harlequin tiles, trying to keep my thoughts on the rhythm of the crutches. I imagined my father and the girl watching me as I hobbled down the hall. I was grateful for the refuge of the elevator. As I rode up to my floor I pictured him paying her and her stuffing the five oversized hundred-franc notes in her dimpled leather purse, a brief motherly indulgence crossing her face.

When I went into my room I put my crutches in the corner and began to think where I should wait for her. The bed seemed premature. The desk falsely studious. That left the couch so I sank into its feathers, nervous and dry mouthed. When she knocked I pulled myself up holding on to the table and dragged my broken leg to the door to let her in. She entered with a faint scent of cigarettes and magnolia blossoms. Pausing in front of me, she said, '*Mais tu es un enfant. Quel âge as-tu*?' she asked. '*Quinze ans, mademoiselle*,' I answered sheepishly. '*Mais pour quinze ans t'es pas beaucoup*,' she answered, not believing fifteen years fit my size. She looked at the cast on my leg. '*Comment as-tu fait ça*?' she asked, pointing toward my cast with her chin as she led me to the sofa, her hand around my waist, guiding me down next to her. '*C'est ta première fois*?' she asked. Anxious and muddled, I wasn't sure whether she was referring to my first broken leg or the first time I had been alone with a woman. '*Oui, ç'est la première fois*,' I admitted. She smiled, obviously interpreting my answer as if it were the latter question and the more interesting one. 'Well, this is the first time I have been with a boy with his leg in a cast so we are both virgins tonight,' she said, and smiled at me.

———

Michael Wolff
+ his father Lewis Wolff

Silent Fathers

When my father was twenty-nine and his father sixty-four they stopped speaking to each other and never would again. When I was twelve, at the bas mitzvah of a cousin, I took matters into my own hands and tried to make my grandfather's acquaintance: 'I'm your oldest grandson.'

'Did your father put you up to this?' said Morris, my grandfather, scowling and turning away. Those are the only words I ever heard him speak, so they've burned hotly, and, as well, have been cause for great puzzlement.

They seemed to imply that my father was a provocateur, or a man with a grudge, one who might use a child for underhanded motives. My father Lewis was in fact deeply conflict averse, a figure of great mildness, bemusement and even contentedness. So much so that he appeared to have wholly let go of the enmity with his father, and, therefore, seemed never to have the need, or interest, to dwell on or explain its meaning or origin. When on the many occasions I sought a more detailed understanding of the family fissure, some context, some gossip, some effort to reveal the protagonists in their full passion – Morris vs Lewis – my father would say from behind the wheel of one of the succession of Buicks he owned, me at his side, 'Morris is crazy, that's all.'

The specific *raison d'être* for the breach was my father's marriage to my mother, a non-Jew. But Morris could hardly have been a zealot. He was a third-generation American living in Paterson, N.J., who attended, sporadically, a conservative temple, observant only at his own convenience.

Yes, no doubt, there was cultural and generational tinder here. But on the day of his wedding my father was still living at home, on that morning had breakfast with his father and mother. My grandparents appear in the wedding pictures, albeit having snubbed the ceremony and only showed up for the reception: Morris and Rose, him with wide tie, her with big brooch.

$\rightarrow$

Michael Wolff is an essayist and author who writes frequently about the media and culture. Born in 1953, his columns have appeared in *Vanity Fair*, *New York Magazine*, *The Guardian*, British *GQ* and *USA Today*. He is the author of five books, including *The Man Who Owns the News*, a biography of Rupert Murdoch, and *Burn Rate*, a memoir of the rise and fall of his internet business. He lives in New York City.

So, an amount of upset, harsh words, tears, but an epochal breach? There are wives, and mothers, and siblings – my father and his brother always remained close – to mitigate such family contretemps. There are children born to start things afresh. And proximity makes most lines in the sand silly after a while. All their lives they never lived more than fifteen minutes apart, my father and his.

What do I not know? About the facts? About my father's character? About what greater force sustained this rift?

A disturbed stubbornness and irrational resolve was always ascribed to my grandfather. As children, and particularly as adolescents, when my brother and sister and I were sullen, withdrawn, implacable in our grievances, my mother would chide, often not too gently, 'Don't pull a Morris.' This had the effect of both making the man Dybbuk-like to us, our evil spirit, and to suggest that we could, if not vigilant, surface the family flaw.

Once, on the many times I further pressed my father to explain again – I was asking him of course to explain himself – he said, 'We had business differences.' 'What business differences could they have had?' My mother said, impatiently, when I pressed her about this after my father had died.

But perhaps I can guess, or infer. My father, a Depression Jew, with one semester of college and four years as a sergeant in the army, stationed, improbably, in India for most of the Second World War, had come home to Paterson, and, after a brief stint selling women's shoes, started – without as far as I can figure an iota of relevant experience – an advertising agency, quite an outlier notion, which, somewhat miraculously, was to grow and prosper.

I can imagine that from a parental perspective this might initially have seemed an ill-advised if not whacky plan. So Morris, hardly a business genius, likely counselled against, disapproved – and felt threatened and miffed when Lewis flaunted his advice. It was not perhaps business so much that was at issue, but change. His son's leap into modernity and what might have seemed like a *goyishe* future, above his station, was a breach, and a put down.

My father's pursuit, I see now, was for the new. However mild and phlegmatic, he was yet propelled forward. The great modern revision and realignment that was to transform so much of the time and culture was not going to leave him out. Such ambitions and predilections, perhaps with an amount of guilt about them, likely made for a complex and perhaps not so well-handled negotiation with a difficult parent. Perhaps the new was only possible by separating from the old and suspicious and doubtful. That must have hurt Morris, as it would any father.

Certainly I have had enough break-ups to know that simply not speaking can be an effective last defence. It's a strange power, like an anorexic's ability not to eat. You might feel helpless but you certainly have this power: silence.

Still, as a father myself, it becomes ever harder to understand. For how long is it possible not to talk to your children? How much suffering can a parent endure? But, at the same time, as a father of adult children, it is not that hard to get. It could happen, I realize, like that. Such anger, and unaccounted resentments, and shifting of the power equation, that, if not gently and expertly finessed, might go somewhere rough and unintended. I have to tell myself often now, the road is long, the game is perilous.

Curiously, my father died just at the point in my life that he stopped speaking to his father in his life. My conversations with my silent father continued, continue now, daily, so much left unsaid, so much more to know, so many questions yet to pose. Did my father continue to address, beseech, argue with, look for comfort and approval from, his old man in the years of silence? I must ask him.

————

Humphrey Stone
+ his father Reynolds Stone

I once stood stock still with my father for half an hour watching a praying mantis. He was by then in the final decade of his life. From early on in my childhood he loved sharing with me this delight in observing closely the natural world, particularly smaller creatures like spiders. He liked studying their behaviour. An early memory is of a robin feeding off his hand during the cold winter of 1947. Birds have been my passion ever since. Iris Murdoch, a close friend who understood him profoundly, described beautifully his character in her address at his memorial service: 'Reynolds never ceased to view the world with a childlike attentive wonder, the equivalent in the artist of the perpetual wonder of the philosopher. He was in his way a philosopher, a total reflective being, unconventional, unworldly, generous in his admiration of others and unambitious except for the true ambition, which is the love of perfection.'

My father was modest and unassuming by nature but with strong convictions. He never imposed his views on me, which ironically made them all the more powerful. With subtlety he drew you into his private world in much the same way as his art does to the viewer. This world didn't include learning about money nor any help making decisions; my mother supplied the necessary common sense and decisiveness. He wasn't the kind of father who kicked a ball around with his son – a pity, as I was a sporty boy – but we were temperamentally alike. Unlike fathers in those days he always greeted me with a hug. He was very tactile, unlike my mother. He would stroke the bark of a tree, as trees came a close third in his loves after his wife and children! We would chuckle a lot over silly jokes and couldn't resist making awful puns, like 'very Bulbankian' to describe a secret rocky crag enveloped in trees. (Bull Banks is from *The Tale of Mr Toad*.) We went for long walks to explore hidden Dorset valleys, preferably with a ruin covered in ivy, and ate many a picnic in a churchyard, the scruffier the better – he designed over a hundred tombstones as it happens – or

Humphrey Stone was born in 1942 in Dorset, England. He is the son of Reynolds Stone, the wood-engraver, designer, painter, book illustrator and letter-cutter in stone, who is best known for his wood engraving and the Roman capitals design of the *Times* masthead and clock and the coat of arms on UK passports. Humphrey is a freelance book designer who has worked at Chatto & Windus and Weidenfeld & Nicolson and as art director at Stanford and Compton Press, Wiltshire. He is married to paper-marbler Solveig Stone. They have four daughters.

Humphrey and Reynolds Stone, 1964
Stone private collection

→

swam at nearby Chesil Beach. Back at home in his cosy old rectory he liked nothing better than to noiselessly slip off his work bench and pull down a book to point out to me a detail of typography or illustration.

Loving company as he did he actually chose to work in the sitting room. We children were banned from disturbing him when we were young, but his powers of concentration were extraordinary. Sylvia Townsend-Warner described the scene thus:

> He works at one end of a large room, walled with books, corniced with stuffed birds in glass cases. He works at a massive table matted with every variety of confusion & untidiness, graving minutely on a small block. The other end of the room is a turmoil of wife, children, distinguished visitors, people dropping in … He likes to work amid a number of conversations he needn't attend to, he likes to feel people within touching distance of his glass case.

This civilized scene hardly reflects a fraught Edmund Gosse-like childhood. It all sounds too good to be true. The truth is I can't remember ever crossing swords with my father, though he did violently lose his temper on occasion, and that was likely to be provoked, for example, by someone cutting down a holly tree. With my mother supplying the spontaneous fun and activities, my parents created a place that became an irresistibly stimulating rural haven for their friends.

Of course a son might long to emulate this dream but it is dangerous to live in one's parents' shoes. If I grew up in his shadow respecting and loving him, it was an inspiring and benign shadow, even if it meant being oversensitive to one's surroundings and an obsessive perfectionist as a typographer. Despite longing to be a farmer I became a book designer, and one who miraculously lives in the country. We could happily now talk fonts and type sizes. At one point he replied in a letter after I expressed worry about my work: 'Don't look over your shoulders. If you think it is right it will be right.' This advice came from a man who was always true to himself.

I was lucky enough to have a father who encouraged me to appreciate the nobility of trees, the structure of landscape, the shape of letters and the physical nature of an object, be it a pebble or a bird's feather.

———

FERNS, wood engraving by Reynolds Stone

Salman Rushdie
+ his father Anis Ahmed Rushdie

Anis was a godless man – still a shocking statement to make in the United States, though an unexceptional one in Europe, and an incomprehensible idea in much of the rest of the world, where the thought of *not believing* is hard even to formulate. But that was what he was, a godless man who knew and thought a great deal about God. The birth of Islam fascinated him because it was the only one of the great world religions to be born within recorded history, whose prophet was not a legend described and glorified by 'evangelists' writing a hundred years or more after the real man lived and died, or a dish recooked for easy global consumption by the brilliant proselytizer St Paul, but rather a man whose life was largely on the record, whose social and economic circumstances were well known, a man living in a time of profound social change, an orphan who grew up to become a successful merchant with mystical tendencies, and who saw, one day on Mount Hira near Mecca, the Archangel Gabriel standing upon the horizon and filling the sky and instructing him to 'recite' and thus, slowly, to create the book known as the Recitation: *al-Qur'an*.

This passed from the father to the son: the belief that the story of the birth of Islam was fascinating because it was an event *inside history*, and that, as such, it was obviously influenced by the events and pressures and ideas of the time of its creation; that to historicize the story, to try to understand how a great idea was shaped by those forces, was the only possible approach to the subject; and that one could accept Muhammad as a genuine mystic – just as one could accept Joan of Arc's voices as having genuinely been heard by her, or the revelations of St John the Divine as being that troubled soul's 'real' experiences – without needing also to accept

Salman Rushdie was born in Bombay in 1947 and is the acclaimed author of eleven novels: *Grimus*, *Midnight's Children* (Best of the Booker award 2008 for the best novel to have won the prize in its first forty years), *Shame*, *The Satanic Verses*, *Haroun and the Sea of Stories*, *The Moor's Last Sigh*, *The Ground Beneath Her Feet*, *Fury*, *Shalimar the Clown*, *The Enchantress of Florence* and *Luka and the Fire of Life* – and one book of stories, *East, West*, as well as four works of non-fiction – including, most recently, *Joseph Anton, A Memoir*. His books have been translated into over forty languages.

Salman Rushdie with his father
Anis Ahmed Rushdie, Bombay
Rushdie private collection

→

that, had one been standing next to the Prophet of Islam on Mount Hira that day, one would also have seen the archangel. Revelation was to be understood as an interior, subjective event, not an objective reality, and a revealed text was to be scrutinized like any other text, using all the tools of the critic, literary, historical, psychological, linguistic and sociological. In short, the text was to be regarded as a human artefact and thus, like all such artefacts, prey to human fallibility and imperfection. The American critic Randall Jarrell famously defined the novel as 'a long piece of writing that has something wrong with it'. Anis Rushdie thought he knew what was wrong with the Quran; it had become, in places, jumbled up.

According to tradition, when Muhammad came down from the mountain he began to recite – he himself was perhaps illiterate – and whichever of his close companions was nearest would write down what he said on whatever came to hand (parchment, stone, leather, leaves and sometimes, it's said, even bones). These passages were stored in a chest in his home until after his death, when the Companions gathered to determine the correct sequence of the revelation; and that determination had given us the now canonical text of the Quran. For that text to be 'perfect' required the reader to believe (a) that the archangel, in conveying the Word of God, did so without slip-ups – which may be an acceptable proposition, since archangels are presumed to be immune from errata; (b) that the Prophet, or, as he called himself, the Messenger, remembered the archangel's words with perfect accuracy; (c) that the Companions' hasty transcriptions, written down over the course of the twenty-three-year-long revelation, were likewise error-free; and finally (d) that when they got together to arrange the text into its final form, their collective memory of the correct sequence was also perfect.

Anis Rushdie was disinclined to contest propositions (a), (b) and (c). Proposition (d), however, was harder for him to swallow, because as anyone who read the Quran could easily see, several *suras*, or chapters, contained radical discontinuities, changing subject without warning, and the abandoned subject sometimes cropped up unannounced in a later *sura* that had been, up to that point, about something else entirely. It was Anis's long-nurtured desire to unscramble these discontinuities and so arrive at a text that was clearer and easier to read. It should be said that this was not a secret or furtive plan; he would discuss it openly with friends over dinner.

There was no sense that the undertaking might create risks for the revisionist scholar, no frisson of danger. Perhaps the times were different, and such ideas could be entertained without fear of reprisals; or else the company was trustworthy; or maybe Anis was an innocent fool. But this was the atmosphere of open enquiry in which he raised his children. Nothing was off limits. There were no taboos. Everything, even holy writ, could be investigated and, just possibly, improved.

He never did it. When he died no text was found among his papers. His last years were dominated by alcohol and business failures and he had little time or inclination for the hard grind of deep Quranic scholarship. Maybe it had always been a pipe dream, or empty, whisky-fuelled big talk. But it left its mark on his son. This was Anis's second great gift to his children: that of an apparently fearless scepticism, accompanied by an almost total freedom from religion. There was a certain amount of tokenism, however. The 'flesh of the swine' was not eaten in the Rushdie household, nor would you find on their dinner table the similarly proscribed 'scavengers of the earth and the sea'; no Goan prawn curry on this dining table.

There were those very occasional visits to the Idgah for the ritual up-and-down of the prayers. There was, once or twice a year, fasting during what Indian Muslims, Urdu- rather than Arabic-speaking, called *Ramzán* rather than Ramadan. And once, briefly, there was a *maulvi*, a religious scholar, hired by Negin to teach her heathen son and daughters the rudiments of faith. But when the heathen children revolted against the *maulvi*, a pint-sized Ho Chi Minh lookalike, teasing him so mercilessly that he complained bitterly to their parents about their disrespect for the great sanctities, Anis and Negin just laughed and took their children's side.

The *maulvi* flounced off, never to return, muttering imprecations against the unbelievers as he went, and after that there were no further attempts at religious instruction. The heathen grew up heathenish and, in Windsor Villa at least, that was just fine.

———

From *Joseph Anton: A Memoir* (Random House, 2012)

Richard Serra
+ his father Tony Serra

One of my earliest recollections is that of driving with my father, as the sun was coming up, across the Golden Gate Bridge. We were going to Marine Shipyard, where my father worked as a pipe fitter, to watch the launching of a ship. This was on my birthday in the fall of 1943. I was four.

When we arrived, the black, blue and orange steel-plated tanker was in weigh, balanced up on a perch. It was disproportionately horizontal and to a four-year-old it was like a skyscraper on its side. I remember walking the arc of the hull with my father, looking at the huge brass propeller, peering through the stays. Then, in a sudden flurry of activity, the shoring props, beams, planks, poles, bars, keel blocks, all the dunnage was removed, the cables released, shackles dismantled, the come-alongs unlocked. There was a total incongruity between the displacement of this enormous tonnage and the quickness and agility with which the task was carried out. As the scaffolding was torn apart, the ship moved down the chute towards the sea; there were the accompanying sounds of celebration, screams, foghorns, shouts, whistles. Freed from its stays, the logs rolling, the ship slid off its cradle with an ever-increasing motion.

It was a moment of tremendous anxiety as the oiler en route rattled, swayed, tipped and bounced into the sea, half submerged, to then raise and lift itself and find its balance. Not only had the tanker collected itself, but so did the witnessing crowd as the ship went through a transformation from an enormous obdurate weight to a buoyant structure, free, afloat and adrift.

My awe and wonder of that moment remains. All the raw material that I needed is contained in the reserve of this memory.

Tony Serra
Serra private collection

Richard Serra was born in San Francisco in 1938. He studied at the University of California (Berkeley and Santa Barbara) and at Yale. He has lived in New York since 1966. Serra's work has been shown in numerous museum exhibitions around the world, including solo exhibitions at the Stedelijk Museum, Amsterdam (1977), Centre Georges Pompidou, Paris (1984) and The Museum of Modern Art, New York (1986 and 2007). In April 2014 Richard Serra installed a major permanent landscape sculpture in the desert of the Brouq Nature Reserve in western Qatar.

John Banville
+ his father Martin Banville

I never saw my father running. This odd fact came to me one day recently when I was sprinting for a train, and I brooded on it for a long time afterwards. He must have run, of course, sometimes and on some necessary occasions, but if he did, and if I saw him, I have no memory of it. His life, moving at an even and unruffled pace, was limited on all sides by the circumstances of his time, his class and his age. There was, really, nowhere that he needed to run to.

Thinking back on the lives of one's parents and making comparisons with one's own life can be a dizzying exercise. It startles me to realize that when my father was the age that I am now, past my middle sixties, he was already long retired and preparing with more or less equanimity for his dotage. My mother was more resistant to the encroachment of age and its attendant enfeeblement – she was in her late fifties when with a great deal of nerve and some panache she purchased her first pair of what in those days were called slacks. My father was thoroughly bemused and, I suspect, more than a little alarmed.

The slacks were my mother's timid gesture towards the Women's Movement that began in the 1960s, and no doubt my father's response was typical of that of a great many of his male contemporaries to the prospect of having their power threatened – as it was to turn out, they need not have worried, or not much, anyway.

Folk then were barely into their forties when they began to complain of feeling old. When I was young myself I did not think of my parents as young or old. To me they seemed, until their final years, to be of an indeterminate age, creatures essentially of a different species, permanent and unchanging, simply there. I do not remember registering signs of their ageing, even when I had left home and made increasingly infrequent return visits. They were, for me, stranded in a timeless zone, preserved in the aspic of what had begun to be The Past.

John Banville was born in 1945. His novels include *The Book of Evidence*, *The Infinities* and, most recently, *Ancient Light*. In 2005 he was awarded the Man Booker Prize for his novel *The Sea*. He has won the Franz Kafka Prize and the Asturias Award 2014. He writes crime novels under the pen-name Benjamin Black, the latest of which is *Holy Orders*.

In her more exasperated moments my mother would say of my father that he was born old. This was not a fair judgment. What made him seem prematurely elderly, was, I think, the narrow range of his expectations, He worked all his life at a white-collar job in a large garage that supplied motor parts to much of County Wexford, but, ironically, he never learned to drive. He was a fast walker, though, and if I concentrate I can hear again the particular syncopated rhythm of his cleated shoe-heels on the pavement outside our house.

In the morning he would walk to work, which took him some twenty minutes. At lunchtime – he called it dinnertime – he would walk home, eat a meal, read the newspaper for a quarter of an hour, then walk back to work. Finishing at six, he would cross the road from the garage to his brother's pub to drink a pint of Guinness before setting off for home and his tea.

Over nearly forty years, this schedule hardly varied, except in the summer months when the family moved to the seaside and he commuted morning and evening by train. At the time I too accepted the daily round, and how much the monotony of it contributed to a sense in him of lost opportunities and made him feel 'old before his time'. For him, as for so many of his class and period, life had its fixed phases: childhood, the brief flowering of adolescence, then adulthood, marriage and the long plateau stretching to retirement.

Perhaps I am being patronizing by thinking my father's life monotonous. What for me would have been a killing dullness may for him have been a comfort, and may have seemed preferable to the vain strivings that tormented so many others around him, my mother included.

I left home when I was seventeen, shaking the dust of Wexford from my heels and heading for what I took to be the bright lights of Dublin. It must have been a wrench for my parents to see me go, so nonchalantly and with hardly a backward glance. I was the last of their children, and now the household, that once had numbered five, was reduced to its original two. They were both dead before I was thirty-five. I mourned them, of course, but how much of my mourning was for them, and how much of it was a first real inkling of my own suddenly all-too-plausible

$\rightarrow$

mortality? It was not that I began to feel old at that moment, but at last I could no longer ignore the fact that I was a grown-up, and that life for grown-ups has only one direction, which is, in the words of Philip Larkin, 'down Cemetery Road'.

In their going my parents were as considerate and as diffident as they had been in life. My mother died of a heart attack while feeding the birds in her garden one gloriously golden afternoon in September; she was sixty-eight, the same age that I am now. A few years later, when he was in his early seventies, my father faded quietly away in a nursing home. When I heard of his death I remember thinking: I am an orphan now. I felt impossibly young, as young as I was when I lived with my parents, yet also immensely older. It was unsettling to realize that from now on, when reference was made to 'Mr Banville', it would be me that was meant. The older generation had departed, leaving me in charge.

W.H. Auden used to say that no matter what the age of the people around him, he always felt he was the youngest person in the room. I too feel that, despite my greying locks. Will I ever fully grow up? My children, of course, though unknowingly, make me aware of my advancing years. How fresh their skin is, how pure the whites of their eyes. These are the things the old notice about the young.

Yet the young, too, carry the past with them. My daughter, who is seventeen and a last child, as I was, drinks endless cups of tea, just as my mother did. Also, she prefers to walk to school rather than going on the bus. One day recently I watched her setting off into the morning's wintry murk and thought there was something familiar about her gait – she walks rapidly, somewhat favouring her left side and turning her left foot outwards at each step. Who was it, I wondered, that walked like that? It was only when I turned away and heard the quick, syncopated rhythm of her heels on the pavement that I suddenly heard in memory my own father's footsteps, walking away. The dead haunt us in the forms of the living, and whisper to us of what the future holds.

———

Chris Blackwell
+ his father Joseph Blackwell

Chris Blackwell with his father, Major Joseph
Blackwell, on an island picnic in Clew Bay
Blackwell private collection

Chris Blackwell was born in England in 1937 and grew up between England and Jamaica. His mother is Blanche Lindo, who comes from a prominent Jamaican family and married Joseph Blackwell of the Crosse & Blackwell family: they divorced when Chris was twelve years old. Major Blackwell had summered in Ireland for many years and he later moved permanently to the West of Ireland (where this photograph is taken). Major Blackwell died in 1993 and is buried on an island in Clew Bay. Islands are in the Blackwell blood: Chris founded Island Records and introduced Bob Marley and reggae music to a worldwide audience. Today he runs Island Outpost, which promotes an alternative luxury lifestyle in Jamaica. Amongst the family's properties is GoldenEye, the former home of Ian Fleming who wrote all the Bond novels there. Fleming was the lover of Blanche Blackwell.

Graydon Carter
+ his father E.P. Carter

My father was a man who got mixed reviews for his overall execution of the Manly Arts. Outdoors, he was on good form. He was a superb skier, a decent sailor, and he played a scratch game of golf. Indoors, things got a bit thicker. He was a hopeless carpenter and general handyman. My mother used to complain that he couldn't even load a dishwasher properly. If he had a specific talent in the Domestic Manly Arts, it was in the arena of farting. He was to the perfectly executed release of air what Constable was to the movement of paint on canvas. My father was a virtuoso and could produce something resembling a tune on command. In my parents' circle, he achieved minor – I won't say celebrity – let's just say notoriety for his gifts in this arena. When we were kids, he would signal the arrival of trouble by asking one of us to pull on his little finger.

My mother grew up in a smart neighborhood of Toronto, then still a sleepy outpost of post-Edwardian probity and caution. She was a well-known local beauty, and during the war had been going out with the captain of the University of Toronto football team. The competition for her hand was not inconsiderable. My father, who had just appeared on the scene, had any number of debits on his ledger. He was the son of a fur trapper who had uprooted his family from London to the wilds of western Canada after reading *The Call of the Wild*. And my father, who was a bit over six feet tall, weighed in at just 115 pounds. On the credit side, he was a Royal Canadian Air Force pilot, and this being wartime, he was in uniform, and he looked good in it. With his moustache and general manner, from a distance he could have passed for an anaemic David Niven.

One evening early in their courtship, he took my mother to the movies at a theatre near her parents' house. They settled into their seats and chatted while the theatre began to fill up, largely with friends of my mother and her family. People said hello. Fellow soldiers saluted one another. And then while the lights were still on and before the newsreel had started, my father did the unthinkable. He broke wind. Not just broke wind, but created a prolonged disturbance that stopped people talking. Heads turned in my parents' direction. My father, never one to do the expected, drew himself up, looked down on my mother and said 'Oh, Margaret!' And with that he edged his way along the row of fellow moviegoers toward the aisle and marched out of the theatre.

My mother, God bless her, found it funny. They spent more than half a century together and in all that time, I never really heard them exchange a stern word, save for the time my father wanted to name their new sloop *Passing Wind*. That was one of the few times my mother put her foot down.

Graydon Carter was born in Toronto in 1949 and has been the editor of *Vanity Fair* since 1992. His tenure at the magazine has taken him through seven presidential administrations and four trouser sizes.

Bill Clinton
+ his father William Jefferson Blythe Jnr

My father, William Jefferson Blythe Jnr, passed away three months before I was born – killed in a car accident on the way to pick up my pregnant mother in Arkansas and bring her back to their new home in Chicago. He was thrown from his car into a ditch on a slick highway in a rainstorm. Knocked unconscious, he was unable to save himself from drowning.

Of course, my mother made sure I knew about my father, and knew how much he had loved her and would have loved me had fate not made other plans for us. But I always yearned to know more, and I have spent my life trying to build a fuller picture of him through mementos and stories shared by people who knew him.

Though I spent my childhood with an idealized image of my father that would in later years be both clouded and enhanced by what I learned, I always missed the most important person I never met.

When I became a father myself, I tried to remember that it was my most important job, one I wanted to do well for the daughter I adore and a lost father who was denied life's greatest gift.

William Jefferson Clinton was born on 19 August 1946, in Hope, Arkansas. President Clinton was the first Democratic president in six decades to be elected twice – first in 1992 and then in 1996. After leaving the White House, President Clinton established the Clinton Foundation with the mission to improve global health and wellness. In 2013, to recognize the contributions of Secretary Clinton and Chelsea, the Foundation was renamed the Bill, Hillary & Chelsea Clinton Foundation. In addition to his Foundation work, President Clinton has served as the top United Nations envoy for the Indian Ocean tsunami recovery effort and as the UN Special Envoy to Haiti. He and his wife, Secretary Hillary Rodham Clinton, have one daughter, Chelsea, and live in Chappaqua, New York.

Ed Victor
+ his father Jack Victor

Sometime in July 1987, on the night before my dad was due to have colon cancer surgery in Los Angeles, I phoned from London to wish him good luck. He was very cheerful, saying that Ronald Reagan had survived it, so why shouldn't he? As a way of distracting him, I told him I was having dinner with Ava Gardner the next night. 'How? Why?' he wanted to know.

I said that Ava was writing her memoirs and had appointed me her literary agent, so we were having dinner to discuss strategy. 'Be careful, son,' he said. 'Why do you say that, Dad?' I asked. 'She might try to seduce you!'

For my father, Ava would always be the ultimate seductress, the gorgeous, eternally sexy Barefoot Contessa. He couldn't know (and wouldn't have wanted to know) that she was now an older lady with white hair who had suffered a bad stroke. But I remember being so touched that, after all this time, he was still worrying about his son, now nearly fifty years old.

As it turned out, my father fell into a coma right after the operation and died one month later without ever waking up. 'Be careful, son' were among his very last words to me.

Ed Victor was born in New York in 1939. He has been living in London for the past fifty years. He was educated at Dartmouth College, then did a M.Litt. at Cambridge before starting in publishing. He worked for Weidenfeld & Nicolson, Jonathan Cape and Alfred A. Knopf before establishing his own literary agency in 1976 with an enviable client list. He represents the estates of Douglas Adams, Iris Murdoch, Raymond Chandler, Irving Wallace and Stephen Spender. Ed Victor is on the board of trustees of the Hay Literary Festival and is one of the original founding directors of The Groucho Club. He served for many years as vice-chairman of the Almeida Theatre.

John Waters
+ his father John Samuel Waters

Filth Financier

My dad was horrified by my early films, but he paid for them. He first lent me $2500 to finance *Mondo Trasho* in 1969 and once I paid him back I asked for $5000 to make *Multiple Maniacs* in 1970, which I also repaid in two years after distributing the film myself. He never saw these underground features but had read the hostile reviews and knew I was once arrested for 'conspiring to commit indecent exposure' while filming. Maybe he just thought making these films was better than me ending up in prison for some of the crimes I was fictionalizing in my work.

I finally asked him for $12,500 to make *Pink Flamingos* in 1972. He hummed and hawed but finally bit the bullet and gave me the budget. It took me decades to realize how amazingly supportive that was. After all, what parent would be proud that their child made *Pink Flamingos*, a film the press described as the 'one of the most vile, stupid and repulsive films ever made'? When it became a hit, I once again started to pay him back but he said, 'You didn't go to college so don't pay me back this time, use it for your next film. You are now set up in business, but don't ask me again.' Wow. What a great lesson in capitalism.

Forty years later, after he died, I was astounded to hear from my mom that he had saved in his safety deposit box the handwritten ledger of my payments, often fifty or a hundred dollars at a time. Now that's what I call love.

John Waters was born in 1955. He is a film director, author, actor and photographer who resides in Baltimore, Maryland.

(Right) John Waters and his father John Samuel Waters
Waters private collection

Daniel Day-Lewis
+ his father Cecil Day-Lewis

Knowing

I sit my father
On my knee
And bounce him
Till he giggles
Helplessly –
'All the king's horses
And all the king's men.'
I whisper to him sweet
And tenderly, my breath
Tickling his ear,
I stroke his fine head
The thick, silvered hair
Parted just so
(Perfectly on the left)
And I tell him all
The many things,
The many things
He'll need to know.

I sit him next
To me on the bench
Outside a little shop
In Clifton, Connemara –
Candies, CREAM cakes,
Whipped cream ices –
The new tweed hat
I'd just bought him
Snug on his head.
In our hands, each
An ice-cream cone,
He leans forward, elbows
On bare knees, to eat it.
I, half smiling,
Open mouth caught
In the promise of words,
Look out toward the lady
As she takes our picture.

Not long ago
I awoke from a dream –
I'm in my old bedroom
At the top of a silent house,
I know that you're down there
The tumour feeding inside you.
What is he doing, I wonder,
Entombed in his goddamn study?
'You know that you're dying' I yell
Down four flights of stairs.
The house rings and recoils,
Doors shudder in their frames,
'Why don't you talk to me? Please
Tell me the fucking things
That I need to know.'
From where he sits in that room
A thick silence rises
Like dusty grain in a silo
Muting the tuning fork
Muting the birdsong
Crawling upward toward me
And I wait in spent air
To be stifled by a life
Of not knowing.

But this, a happy day
Retreating my dead father
To his childhood
Then reassuring him,
Reassuring him,
Insisting, in the sibilant refrain
Of waves resolving
To sheer, lace-edged
Transparencies,
That all shall be well
That he shall grow strong
And straight and true
And that he'll know,
When the time comes,
Just exactly
What he needs to do.

———

James Dearden
+ his father Basil Dearden

When I was a child I didn't see a lot of my father, mainly because he left the house to go to work early in the morning before I woke up and came back in the evening very near my bedtime. If I was lucky he came up to read me a bedtime story, if I wasn't already asleep. He was also away quite a lot of the time 'on location'.

My father was a film director, which to me seemed perfectly normal. Occasionally I went to see him at work 'on the set' in a big cavernous sound stage where nothing much happened for most of the time until a bell rang for silence. I was allowed to watch from an area near the camera, a hallowed circle of light in the enveloping gloom, where the camera assistant would clap the clapperboard and then my father would call 'Action!' The actors spoke a few lines before my father would call 'Cut!'. It was very boring and I couldn't wait to go home.

My father was a quiet, shy man, so it was quite surprising to see the respect in which he was held at work, where everybody seemed to hang on his every word. He had a reputation as something of a martinet, who didn't suffer fools gladly. But at home he couldn't have been gentler. The only time I ever recall him raising his voice in anger was when, aged about seven, I was experimenting with my chemistry set in my newly redecorated bedroom. I left a glass tube of some chemical to heat over a Bunsen burner, the cork stopper in the tube, with obviously calamitous results when the tube exploded and inky black liquid sprayed all over the room. My father burst in through the door, put me over his knee and administered a couple of half-hearted smacks, for which he promptly apologized. He never raised his hand against me again.

I was sent away to boarding school at the age of eight, as was the custom in those days. Neither of my parents had been to private school, and I am sure they thought they were doing the right thing, which perhaps they were. I was desperately homesick and longed for the three visits a term that were permitted, which mainly consisted of trundling up and down Brighton Pier in the rain and then retiring to one of the grand but faded seafront hotels to have tea, before the inevitable return to school in time for evening chapel on Sunday. The countdown to 5 pm was

James Dearden began his career making short films, culminating in the 42-minute *Diversion*. It became the basis for the worldwide hit *Fatal Attraction*, for which he received an Academy Award nomination. He has written and directed several other feature films including *Rogue Trader* and *Pascali's Island*, an official entry at the 1988 Cannes film festival. His stage version of *Fatal Attraction* opened at the Theatre Royal Haymarket in March 2014.

My father, Basil, looking pensive.

GP·916

→

91

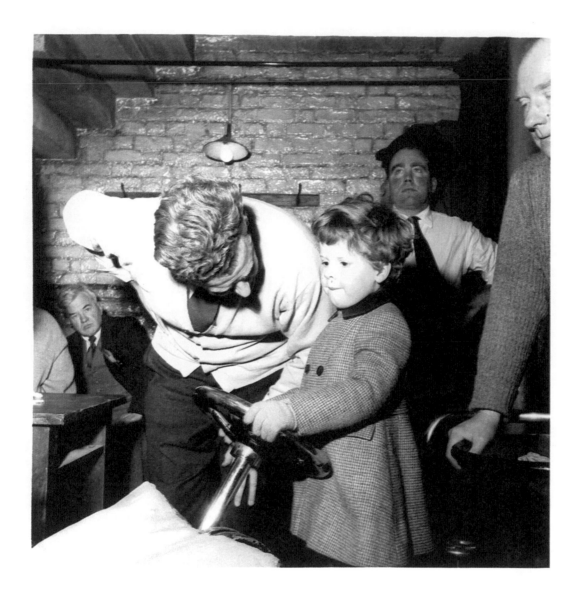

me, aged 3, also looking
pensive on a rare visit to the
set. Note the crew all wearing
collar and tie.

always grim, and my father used to throw a cricket ball high up into the sky for me to catch, right up to the last moment, before the tolling of the chapel bell signalled that the weekend was over and that was the last I would see of him until the next visit some four or five weeks later. That is still my overriding memory of him, throwing the cricket ball for me in those last desperate moments before we had to say goodbye and then
I stood there watching his car disappearing down the school drive with all the other parents' cars.

So we didn't 'do' a lot together, in the manner of today's fathers and sons. We didn't go on fishing trips, or build things together in the garage, or share a hobby, although he did occasionally take me to watch Chelsea at Stamford Bridge in the days when they were still known as The Pensioners and always seemed to be getting relegated to the Second Division. But I don't think I will ever again feel as close to anyone as I did to my father, or the recipient of such unconditional love. I remember an occasion, which my mother related to me, when I was about eighteen, running across the lawn with shoulder-length hair, and a guest at the house, a businessman friend of one of my uncles, asked my father in a tone of disapproval, 'What do you think when you see your son looking like that?', to which he replied simply, 'Immense love', which must have put an immediate end to the conversation.

I think my father was basically a depressive, and as he got older and his career started to flag, and the gaps between films got longer, I was always worrying about him, sensing a deep sadness. He still went to the studio every day and sat in his office, but he was from an era when a director went from one film to the next, and he was only really happy when he was filming. One night when I was still at university, just after turning twenty-one, I got a shaky voiced phone call from my mother at about ten o'clock at night: 'Darling, I've got bad news. Daddy's been killed in a car crash.' He'd been drinking at the bar at Pinewood before getting into his little blue Mini (he'd recently downsized from a Daimler-Jag to economize) to drive home to London on the M4, apparently fallen asleep at the wheel and veered off the road into one of the motorway columns. I'd like to think it was instantaneous, as the car had burst into flames. My uncle-in-law, Dougie Hayward, one of my father's few close friends, advised me not to go to identify his body and that he would in my place, for which I was grateful, if also a little guilty, feeling I owed it to him to say a proper goodbye.

I was absolutely devastated. I felt very diminished by his death and traumatized by its sudden brutality. It took me years to get over it, if one ever does. He was only sixty and I am already older than him. But part of me will forever be that small boy, waiting for the cricket ball to come back down from the sky.

———

Roddy Doyle
+ his father Rory Doyle

My father lost his teeth in Ballybunion. This happened in August 1966, when I was eight, and – I just worked it out now – my father was forty-two. I sat on the beach for hours and watched him and my sister diving into the water, and coming back up, and diving in and coming back up. This was the Atlantic Ocean they were diving into, so the chances of finding his teeth, or anyone else's, were slim. But, eventually – and inevitably – I heard a roar: he'd found his teeth, or my sister had. He came out of the water a bit like Ursula Andress in *Dr No*, if Ursula had been male and she'd just found the false teeth she'd lost hours earlier.

I don't think my father did it – lost his teeth – deliberately.

I forget what exactly happened, or I never knew. A wave smacked the back of his head and the teeth jumped out. He opened his mouth to speak and a wave lifted him high. When he came back down, the teeth were still up there – then gone – a splash. Something like that. He didn't wade into the Atlantic with the intention of losing his teeth, then finding them. Or, he didn't hide them in his armpit – hiding places were limited – and then pretend to find them. Their loss had been an accident, their recovery a bigger accident.

But sometimes I wondered.

All through his life, right up to the day before he died, my father planted stories. He left a trail of events behind him, things he'd said or done that still made people grin when they told me about them decades later.

'He was a character.'

'He was hilarious.'

'He was a bit mad, your dad.'

'He was a gentleman.'

Roddy Doyle was born in 1958. He has written ten novels, including *The Commitments* (1987), *Paddy Clarke Ha Ha Ha* (Booker Prize 1993), *A Star Called Henry* (1999), and, most recently, *The Guts* (2013). He has also written seven books for children, a memoir of his parents, two collections of short stories, screenplays and stage plays, the most recent being *The Commitments*, at the Palace Theatre, London. *The Second Half*, which he wrote with Roy Keane, was published in October 2014. He lives and works in Dublin.

He was drunk when he met my mother. He made a bad impression, before he came back the next week and made a much better one. It was a better story. When he was serving his time as a printing apprentice, he won a prize for excellence – cash. He went up to Fox's with it, and bought a pipe and plug tobacco, filled the pipe, took his first puff, got sick, and continued smoking. It was as if he'd done it so he could tell us about it forty years later. It was a great story – the tall, skinny boy smoking himself into adulthood. About the same time – 1940 or 1941 – he was standing on Dame Street in thick fog. He had his bike with him but he couldn't cycle home because he couldn't see a thing. He started to walk, and literally bumped into one of his cousins. The cousin brought him slowly up the street to Burdock's and bought him a bag of chips – his first. How long would the rest of us have to stand in fog before a cousin bumped into us? Every time I buy chips I think of my father.

That's the point.

My mother told me about the time they were at a party to celebrate a missionary priest's fifty years in the priesthood. A bishop had just been praising the priest – what a wonderful man he was and an example to everyone. My father stood up and walked across the room and, a minute later, she heard the burst of laughter. He'd gone straight up to the bishop and, pointing at the priest, he'd said, 'If he's so wonderful, how come you're the bishop?' The roomful of people went home with that one.

He had a triple bypass in 1992, and was delighted to wake up alive. He chatted away, his head a mix of what he heard on the radio and the hallucinations that kept visiting him for weeks after the surgery. He was asking me about the football scores he'd missed while he was 'under the knife', when he looked out at the hospital corridor, and said, 'That black man's very skinny for a chicken.' There was no black chicken man but, nevertheless, he became part of the family. He still delivers the eggs.

$\rightarrow$

The evening before he died last March, he'd been moved to a different ward. He was disorientated; he wasn't sure where he was. He didn't seem able to see. He could make out light – the last of the day's sunlight – but he couldn't understand why it was in that particular position. It didn't upset him. He knew my mother was there. There was one other bed in the room, about to be occupied by an elderly man who sat in the chair beside it. He was being asked a series of questions by a nurse, a routine he'd obviously been through already.

'Are you a married man, Michael?'

'My wife is dead.'

We sat listening. My father seemed to be sleeping; his eyes were closed.

'Do you have any children?'

'I have three sons.'

'What is the name of the eldest son?'

'I said it already. Michael. Same as myself.'

'So he is your next of kin.'

'Yes.'

'What is the name of your second-eldest son?'

The man hesitated.

'Kevin,' said my father.

'Kevin,' said the man.

My father died the next day. He was ninety. I haven't met a Kevin since. When I do, I'll grin. I might cry too.

———

James Dyson
+ his father Alec Dyson

My father said goodbye, holding a small leather suitcase as we waved from the back door. He set off to Holt station and caught the steam train that ferried him to London. That was the last time I saw him. His brave cheerfulness chokes me every time I recall the scene.

My elder brother Tom, my mother and I were drinking asparagus soup when the phone rang. As my mother answered the call, I had a naive premonition of the news. This was surprising since I was unaware that cancer was an inevitable killer in the 1950s. A grim sadness fell. We feared for our talented elder sister Shanie, who was away at boarding school. How would she take the news on her own?

Tom and I, eleven and nine, were lucky to be day pupils at the local Greshams School where my father had been head of the classics department. Logie Bruce-Lockhart with his kind wife Jo was the generous headmaster. They arranged for us to become boarders at a nominal fee, as this would allow my mother to go out to work. In fact she trained as a teacher and later went stoically up to Cambridge as a mature student to take a degree in English.

I'm not sure that boarding was a good idea. I had no choice but to shut down my emotions and imagine I would always be scarred and alone – a need perhaps to prove something to a lost parent, or just a survival technique.

It is impossible to imagine my father's wild and heart-rending emotions as he was saying goodbye to us, knowing that he might die 120 miles away in Westminster Hospital. All the more tragic as he had just spent the Second World War fighting in Burma, a very long sea voyage away from his young bride and family.

I remember him as an ever-cheerful polymath. He ran the school cadet force as a major (he was twice Mentioned in Dispatches in wartime), coached hockey and rugger, and taught me to sail dinghies on the Norfolk Broads. He used to wake me

$\rightarrow$

James Dyson was born in Norfolk, England, in 1947. He is a British inventor, industrial designer and founder of the Dyson company. He invented the Dual Cyclone bagless vacuum cleaner.

up early in the morning to catch the spring tide. He did so following a stormy night in 1954 – the sea floods had swept across the valleys of north Norfolk. This wasn't simply a matter of jumping in the car. Our car, a Standard 12, powered, I recall, by a Jaguar engine, demanded a hand-crank start with a violent kickback and had frequent breakdowns. All an adventure.

My father played the tenor recorder in a group, produced school plays (I still have his margin notes in miniature volumes of Shakespeare) and was happy pouring molten lead to cast miniature soldiers and working wood in his workshop. He wrote a children's book about India, which he illustrated with charming watercolours. It was called *The Prince and the Magic Carpet*. Happily my grandchildren love me reading it to them and chime in with the magic words 'Dhurry dhurry ooper jow' to set the carpet flying. He was able to spout spontaneous and suggestive limericks. He was an amateur photographer who developed his own prints, sticking them into precious albums. He was always doing an activity which involved us, whether it was feeding the chickens, allowing us to stand leaning out from the car's running board or putting stage make-up on the Greshams School actors.

My highly intelligent brother followed my father with a scholarship in classics at Corpus Christi, Cambridge. I showed no such promise in spite of Logie's encouraging remarks when I left school! But I'm sure my father would have been not too disappointed to see me transformed into a design engineer at London's Royal College of Art. He would have been tickled that I used my hands and my brain. I have maintained strong links with Cambridge. There are Alec Dyson postgraduate scholarships in science awarded at Corpus every year and Dyson funds many projects in the wonderful Cambridge engineering department.

When I was eight we were motoring back from Cornwall after what was to be our last holiday together. We stopped for a picnic on Dartmoor. I set off alone along a track exploring in the high bracken. Round a corner I discovered my father being violently sick. Before I could say anything he said 'Don't tell Mummy'. It was typical of him to not want to cause alarm. I felt immense love and compassion for him as we made our way back to be with our family. Sixty years have not softened the horror of these memories. Nor the sadness that he missed enjoying his three children growing up and marrying wonderful people. How he would have relished playing with his grandchildren, of whom there are six.

This is all the more poignant as one of my own grandchildren, Mick, is now the age I was when my father died. Mick is loving, bright as a button and self possessed yet still takes his ruffled soft puppy to bed with him: he is far too vulnerable to lose his father. I realize how much I missed mine as I watch Mick playing ping-pong and doing jigsaws with his creative and loving father, Ian.

———

The Edge
+ his father Garvin Evans

Fishing seems to connect us to a primal existence. The acceptable face of hunting. Somehow it's less obnoxious dragging a fish out of its watery habitat and banging it on the head with a stick then shooting another mammal in a forest with an arrow or bullet.

I remember a fishing trip with my father, Garvin, when I was twelve years old. We went to a river in Wales called the Tywi for three days with Grand-uncle Gordon. It wasn't exactly the passing of the secret knowledge as my dad and I were both pretty clueless, but the important thing was we got to hang out doing something that we could share. It's so long ago that I can't remember much beyond the awareness of a rare bonding time spent with my dad.

There is one moment, however, that is indelibly printed in my memory. It was the electric shock I felt down my spine as my line suddenly went taut, my fishing rod bent downward, and I realized that a large salmon had taken my bait. The next few minutes were a blur of activity that ended in a slack line and no fish. There was a post-mortem of possible causes: a bad knot, the reel resistance set too tight, lack of tension on the line, but the disappointment faded quickly and we moved easily into that time-honoured ritual, the telling of 'the one that got away' story. It was an important time for my father and me but the connection made between boy and nature has also remained.

I still love to go into the wilderness to reconnect with – exactly what I don't know. Maybe the idea of a primal existence and a more natural pace of life, the way my senses are all engaged and heightened, maybe it's to finally catch the one that got away. All I know is that when I had my son it was one of the first things we did together. First hunting for crabs on the rocks then a bit of line fishing and eventually some bigger stuff.

Here we are with a barracuda I caught in the Bahamas. As a father I see now how the secret knowledge gets passed in both directions. My son Levi from the earliest time insisted on throwing back his catch, which now makes sense to me because they are all 'the one that got away'.

The Edge fishing with his son Levi
Edge private collection

The Edge was born David Evans in Essex, England in 1961 to Welsh parents, Garvin and Gwenda Evans, who moved to Ireland when he was an infant. He was a founding member of the rock group U2 in 1976. He is a gifted songwriter and musician with a distinctive guitar style and has also played the piano, keyboards and contributed lead and backing vocals on U2 albums and tours. He is married to Morleigh Steinberg with whom he has two children. The Edge has three daughters from his first marriage.

Robert Fisk
+ his father Bill Fisk

My mother called me in Beirut in 1993 to say that my dad had died. I had long since stopped calling him Dad – Father was the word I used, firstly with a kind of irony because he always demanded respect, and then because it suited his years and his history. He was ninety-three when he died; he was born in 1899, so I can say that my dad – or my father, Bill Fisk – was born in 'the century before last'. He had been a soldier in the Great War, a patriot in the most literal sense of the word. Bill was a faithful man, he kept his word, he paid his bills on time.

In any event, I replied to my mother on the phone that day twenty-one years ago that Bill was 'a man of his time'. He was a Victorian, a poor boy taken from school by his father at thirteen because Edward Fisk – my grandfather, former mate on the *Cutty Sark* and later deputy harbour master of Birkenhead – had no more money to pay for his son's education. So Bill was self-educated in accountancy until, by the time of his retirement in the 1960s, he was borough treasurer of Maidstone. I also told my mother that day of his death that Bill, over the years, had taught me to love books and history. That was his bequest to his son.

It was the best I could say of him. For in his later years, he could be a harsh man – I avoid the word 'cruel' with some difficulty – shouting at my mother and myself, insisting that he and he only would decide where we would live, how we would spend money, what I would wear, what I would say, that I would attend – against my wishes – a violent, bully infested English boarding school. One day, during a fierce argument, he threw a silver-plate knife at me.

Bill had inherited the world of his own father, which was the Mersey of the late 1890s: racist, anti-Irish, intolerant of those who did not share his views. Many years into his retirement, he was appointed to a fair-rent tribunal – and came home one day

Robert Fisk was born in 1946. He is Middle East Correspondent of *The Independent* and lives in Beirut, where he has been based for the past thirty-eight years. Educated in England and Ireland, gaining a Ph.D. in Politics at Trinity College Dublin, he has won eighteen press awards for his coverage of Middle East conflicts and is the author of a number of best-selling books, including *In Time of War*, his Ph.D. study of Irish neutrality during the Emergency, *Pity the Nation*, a first-hand account of the 1975-90 Lebanese civil war and *The Great War for Civilization*, a history memoir of the Middle East from the Great War to the present.

boasting that he had raised the rent of a young couple because he suspected they were not married. He called black people 'Niggers' – and I think this was intended to provoke me.

It did. I did not go to see him before he died. And yet…

I suspect there is always an 'and yet' about out fathers. For Bill was a teenage soldier. He tried to sign up for the British army underage because he wanted to join his schoolmates and fight for 'Little Belgium'. Once he was in uniform, they sent him instead to Dublin because of a man called Padraig Pearse, and he arrived in Ireland after the Rising, posted to Victoria Barracks (now Collins Barracks) in Cork. This saved him from the first Battle of the Somme in 1916, in which 20,000 British soldiers, including some of Bill's school friends, were killed on the first day of the attack. Pearse, I once tried to explain to Bill, probably saved his life – and mine!

Bill arrived in France for the third Somme battle in 1918, fought in the trenches, helped to liberate Cambrai – and was then asked to execute a Royal Artillery soldier by firing squad. The soldier had killed a British military policeman in Paris. Bill refused the order. He would not execute a fellow soldier. It was, I am sure, the finest act of his life, one of which his son would have approved with all his heart. Second Lieutenant Bill Fisk was a courageous man. He had wanted to join the Gurkhas, become a regular officer, but his brave act of disobedience destroyed such hopes. So he lost his military career – and, it seems, a French girlfriend – and returned to the fog of Birkenhead.

And as the years went by, Bill became a disillusioned man. He read the biographies of Field Marshal Haig and realized the Great War was founded upon lies, 'a great waste' was all he would call it when I talked to him one day when he feared (mistakenly) that he was dying of cancer. He stopped attending his church. He became more right wing than the Conservative party he always voted for. In his very old age, he asked my mother to frame a photograph of him in 1918, in uniform and riding a horse called Whitesocks, which, according to his handwriting on the back, was taken near Hazebrouck in Flanders. He wanted to put it on his desk. My mother unkindly refused.

All his life, Bill said he wanted a proud son, but he was unable to understand that affection must be earned and not taken for granted. He said he wanted a son who honoured him. I fear what he really wanted was an obedient junior officer. This he could not have. Which was his misfortune. And, I suppose, mine too.

———

Colin Farrell
+ his father Eamon Farrell

Colin Farrell and his
father Eamon Farrell

Fathers and Sons

I have known this much of death and stood beside myself and watched me die,
The men that we become live somewhere within our father's eye…
And I have watched myself shed skin, watched feather fall,
And looked and wondered, where was the beginning,
Where upon a rising tide, from where, where come we all…

Where does man find himself upon the precipice of change,
Within his father's arms his cooing plea to rearrange,
All that was born to him and came before his fall
I have wondered, wondered, wonder still,
And yet I have no answer, none at all.

Perhaps the laughter shed and tears that graced,
The years hence now have quickened, upped their pace.
That I should, as a man (and boy), still seek to gain,
The answers to my father's joy, his doubts, his pain.
The moments I remember, some were fine,
And others grip me still through all this time.
The struggles of the men who stood before,
The door of fatherhood and pled 'no more'.

Colin Farrell was born in Dublin in 1976. He has been working as an actor, both at home and abroad, for the last twenty years. He has played a variety of characters and has enjoyed every one, but some more than others. In 2009 he won a Golden Globe Award for his performance in Martin McDonough's *In Bruges* and in 2010 he won an Irish Film and Television Award for his performance as Syracuse in Neil Jordan's *Ondine*. He very much enjoys chocolate and cheeseburgers. He is a father and a son.

No more fear and suffering, no more in haste.
The hours, days and months we lay to waste.
How time becomes the crystal that we hold,
So dear next to our breast till we are old.
The clock that ticked anew when my sons came,
The doubt and fear that called itself in vain,
No more the tired lonely fear of 'I',
For hearing my sons weep is me to cry.

To watch now as they reach and grasp and fall,
And rise again and answer their own call.
Not burdened by a past that's mine alone,
As die I die and live anew each morn.

Perhaps we're bound by what is found in light,
While shadows of our kin beget our right,
To climb upon a mountain carved anew,
And say 'I am I my father, you are you'.

So what, I wonder, does this circle bring,
The calling of our hearts as ancients sing,
I have the love that I was given then,
And found the time through my own children's pen.
The colours that they draw upon their world,
Bewitch me with the kindness they unfurl,
Their dreams are mine and my fears die with me,
In dying, I pray death may set all free.

So thank you Father, Son and our shared Ghost,
For trusting in our days to gift us most,
The loving hands that try and fail and try,
Upon this blessed gift that loves not why.
From him to me, and now from me to you,
In all things that we find and seek anew,
Are all the answers to this mystery,
To love is all the why we dream to be…

———

Johnny Flynn
+ his father Eric Flynn

My dad was an anomaly. He came from another era. I felt that, in the time that I knew him, his worldly achievements were all under his belt and put aside. This made room for his own mythology, which was born from an unending seam of stories, songs, philosophy and oddities plucked from his previous lives and bestowed upon us like his gospels.

I begged him to tell me the stories of his childhood in Hong Kong and China again and again, his earliest memories as a prisoner of war in Shanghai, the time he spied on a lady in a bath cubicle and slipped and sliced his leg open … when the Americans liberated the camps and the Red Cross dropped food parcels, some landing on prisoners who'd survived the war to be crushed by the Hershey bars and bananas that would also make the kids like my dad vomit because they'd had nothing to eat but rice and weevils all of their lives. The time he turned down playing James Bond. The night he met my mum and when they decided to get married seven days later up a mountain looking for black eagles. It all came through a fug of smoke and a twinkle in his eye.

It was really good to be riding shotgun with him in any of those bashed-up old cars he had: an Opel Manta (he joined an owners' club), an old Escort van he bought from a neighbour … in his car he was king. Their smell a combination of Hamlet cigar smoke with faint overtones of fishing gear and the whiff of a stale cricket bag … the sound of their juddering engines, sweetened by his Johnny Mercer and big band tapes lovingly copied from vinyl with his illegible scrawl on the labels – I keep finding them stashed in various boxes, there's a pile in my mum's kitchen like a totem to his memory. I told him that one day when I'd made my way in the world I'd buy him an Aston Martin DB7 – we never had a car that was less than fifteen years old, we never owned a house.

My dad was a singer, an actor and a songwriter. I guess his cult was pretty strong because I followed him there and so did three out of my four siblings. We're all trying to do what he did – it's like a comfort blanket. It's scary how often I find myself treading in

Johnny Flynn was born in 1983 in South Africa but brought up in England to escape apartheid. He won a music scholarship to Bedales. He is an actor and musician fronting the folk-rock band Johnny Flynn & The Sussex Wit. He has acted in films including *Lotus Eaters* and starred in stage productions including *Jerusalem* opposite Mark Rylance.

Johnny Flynn and his father Eric Flynn
Flynn private collection

his big footprints, and I wonder how I got here … it's obvious really. My own son, who never knew his grandfather, met him on his first Christmas when we turned on the TV and there was Dad in a ballroom dance routine for a *Two Ronnies* sketch. That's typical, I thought, as I introduced Gabriel to him: showing off with such wry charm.

He was like that – a bit proud. But when his lung cancer developed, something began to shift in him. He'd had a dream on a train about a dark forest full of fear and a tree of life amongst other prophetic symbols and told me about it. That wasn't like him. He'd never once talked about spiritual or supernatural things to me, save for a few fantastic ghost stories. But in another way, I could see that he was becoming his truest self. That is to say, his apparent mortality was forcing his hand, and suddenly he became breathtakingly honest. In his last weeks I remember going to him to hear a certain story for the last time. 'I'm not sure it really happened,' he said when I asked him to tell it. I'd heard it thousands of times though – it was part of my DNA.

'Really Dad? Come on, tell me the story!' I demanded.

He just smiled and said, 'It doesn't really matter though, does it.'

And finally, after hearing his stories and listening to his lectures all of my eighteen years, he was teaching me something really important. The night before he died I was driving back from London with my brother to Wales where my parents lived and we couldn't remember a verse to a lullaby he'd written and sung to all of us kids. Our plan was to extract it from him for posterity. But he'd almost gone by the time we got there.

He died in a state of grace and acceptance that is the privilege of my life to have witnessed. It meant we were sad, but elated to see him so fearless. I feel the best of him in me now and hear his voice come from my mouth every time I sit Gabriel on my knee to sing him a song.

———

Richard Ford
+ his father Parker Carroll Ford

My father was a man who couldn't do many things well. He was the infant child of a suicide father. I've always assumed he'd had no one to teach him. Some boys have fathers who teach them all the important skills – carpentry, fishing, sports, refined things. He didn't. I loved him very much; but so many memories are of acts he set forth to accomplish and somehow failed. Not enormous things, by any means. He worked hard, made a living; loved my mother and me. He was gentle and shy and restrained and happy. Mirthful. It was just the three of us, in Mississippi. All our frailties stood in high relief.

Once, I told him I wanted to be a boxer, and he bought me a punching bag – a speed bag. He built a frame out of discarded wood and fastened it to the wall in our garage. I took a boxer's stance before it, hit the bag once – not so hard – and it all collapsed on the floor. Another time I said I wanted to be a basketball player, had aspirations for the high-school team. Again he found wood – large, heavy planks – and nailed together a backboard, screwed on an iron hoop, erected the whole thing on a long, spliced-together mast in our back yard, It didn't look good. It weighed too much. The wind blew it back and forth. My shots careened off unpredictably. Plus he'd bolted on the hoop at nine feet instead of the regulation ten. He didn't tell me this – if he knew – so what I learned was to shoot at a basket that was too low.

This was the fifties, we lived in the suburbs. There was naturally a lawn. Power mowers were new to us, but we had one. However, he had little luck getting the Briggs & Stratton started. One wound a rope around a metal cylinder on top then pulled it back hard. The engine (supposedly) would 'catch' and roar into life like an old airplane. It appeared fairly simple. Though not simple enough. It all made him furious. He would wind and pull, wind and pull. Then for a while I would. He was a large, fleshy man; being furious and unsuccessful made him seem helpless. Even he knew it. Mowing the grass – which he intended me to do and him to supervise – always occasioned controversy and various shades of anger.

$\rightarrow$

Barbecue was new, as well. The thought that he could roast a chicken on an electric spit using a shiny, aluminum oven-ish grill thing that burned charcoal, purely delighted him. This was to happen on the concrete-slab patio behind the house. He was not, however, a patient man – with barbecues no more than with lawn mowers. Readying the coals took too long, in his view. Plus, there should be constant flames, not black ingots, chemically soaked, turning whitely, slowly hot (as the instructions stated). Soaking the coals more was his solution, which occasioned wild but short-lived upward flamings. For this reason, he started the chicken turning too early – before the coals were right. He wanted it all to be cooked before it could be. His big, soft face, I remember bore a smile of intensity. In the end, we ate our chicken pink against the bone, which caused my mother to say, with some sarcasm, that we would now get a disease uncooked chicken promoted. This made him angry, and we never used the little motor-driven spit again.

He also took me fishing. I don't think he wanted to take me, but I wanted to go (or said I did). And because he travelled during the week, Saturdays were our chance to do such things. He asked and found out about two lakes open to the public – one close, another two hours away. As a boy he must've fished. But we had no gear in our house, no knowledge. He never told stories about fishing

Bee Lake was the one he chose – the farther one away, for the adventure. This was in the extremely hot, extremely buggy and snaky, extremely sun-beaten Mississippi Delta. The famous one. There was a row of rough, airless cabins on a weedy bluff above the lake, which was an old cut-off, a horseshoe, where the Yazoo River had long ago changed its course. Metal boats were for rent, as were long cane poles with hooks and mesh boxes of crickets and paper cups full of damp dirt and worms. This was bait.

The lake was without motion and had grown up in cypress-knees. Snake-doctors and giant mosquitoes and biting horseflies buzzed around us. We could've rented a motor, but that was extravagant for first-timers. We rowed out onto the hot shadeless lake – not too far. We baited our hooks, adjusted our bobbers for where we believed the bottom to be – my father in the back, me in the front. And we fished. And fished, and fished – in the heat and bugs and dense, windless summer air. We had sandwiches and Cokes. These were gone by noon. We moved from one spot to another without any sense of where fish might be, only where they weren't. We put our lines in the water, brought our hooks up, sat and stared and sweated. He smoked, I grew drowsy and stiff. Until we'd used up our crickets and worms, and had not caught a fish – either of us. At a certain hour in the late day, when it's hottest, we simply rowed in without comment. We'd rented one of the cabins for the night – one of the rank, breathless white-wooden boxes with only one window and a table fan. There was no place to go for supper. 'Why don't we go home,' he said, standing in the mud where we'd beached our boat. He had a look on his face. He seemed amused, but wasn't. 'All right,' I said. 'That sounds good enough.' Fishing was over. We went other times – other lakes, deep-sea fishing in the Gulf. I can't remember us ever catching anything. He was no good at it, and neither was I. We had that in common. Father and son.

My wife said to me, musing out my window, after I'd read this all to her, 'The reader's waiting for affection in this, you know.' 'I loved my father,' I said somewhat defensively. 'I said so.' 'Oh, I know,' she said. 'You don't love people for what they can and can't do.' 'No,' I said. 'You love them for other reasons.' Love is a complex business. I'm not the first to testify. Sometimes it's only sensible in the presence of what might seem to be its opposite – but in this case isn't. There's a word for that hard, other thing. Adamant.

Richard Ford was born in Jackson, Mississippi, in 1944. He is the author of eleven books of fiction including the Bascombe trilogy, the *New York Times*-bestselling novel *Canada*, which won the Prix Femina Étranger in France, and most recently, *Let Me Be Frank With You*, a suite of four long stories narrated by Frank Bascombe. He writes frequently for newspapers in the US and abroad. His fiction has been translated into more than twenty-five languages. He is married to Kristina Ford and lives in East Boothbay, Maine.

Gavin Friday
+ his father Robert 'Paschal' Hanvey

My dad passed away in July 2006 and I still miss him, very much. The most likely reason I miss him so much is that I never really got to know my father. I am from that sad generation where a close, expressive, mutually rewarding father-son relationship was a rarity. It was a typical Irish thing back then: a father and a son not really speaking to each other, not really knowing each other. Was I close to him? In all honesty, no. I loved him – craved for his love, but I didn't really know him. To be fair, in his later years there was what you could call an emotional truce between us, where a silent non-verbal communication had developed. Sometimes it was just a look, or a tone of voice. But most frequently was the Dad-will-fix-it persona who suddenly appeared. Many is the time my dad would call up to my house unannounced to 'fix' the blocked sink that in fact wasn't blocked at all, and during his last years he invented countless 'chores' that only he could mend as I was a 'hopeless gobshite that couldn't make a proper cup of tea never mind put a plug on the kettle'. I was blessed to spend some very precious time with him in the last weeks before his death when we spoke for many hours as he lay on trolley in the A&E of the Mater Hospital. He held my hand for the first time in what must have been forty years and he told me how much he loved and respected me. We both made our peace.

**'Old father, old artificer, stand me
now and ever in good stead.'**
James Joyce

Gavin Friday was born Fionan Martin Hanvey in October 1959 in Dublin. He was one of the originators of Lypton Village, the seventies collective that spawned U2 and the Virgin Prunes. Loved and hated in equal parts, the Virgin Prunes (1978-1985) are now seen as one of the iconic legends of the avant-garde post-punk movement. Friday's career, post Virgin Prunes, has been diverse, from his first exhibition of paintings in 1986 to his varied work as an actor: this has included *Ich Liebe Dich*, his 2002 dramatic take on the works of Brecht and Weill, Neil Jordan's *Breakfast on Pluto* in 2005 and *Nothing Like the Sun* with the Royal Shakespeare Company in 2009. Friday has released four solo albums over the last three decades and is a prolific composer in the world of film score, for which he has received three Golden Globe nominations.

Artwork by Gavin Friday

113

Bob Geldof
+ his father Bob Geldof Snr

My father had two pairs of underpants. They were a class of very baggy Y-fronts. The elastic on one of the pairs had gone. Meticulously he would hike them up above his waistband and tie his belt tightly around the Bri-Nylon shirt, the loose washed-too-often-in-a sink vest and the unelasticated top of his flabby undies.

He neither looked nor was hapless. He was simply a man without a woman or money in the early sixties. He'd leave on Monday morning and come back Friday night. We shared a bedroom. It was awkward. But I think he liked it. It gave him a false proximity to the son he hadn't seen all week and really hardly knew except for my hopelessly essayed efforts at being the model child. Until I decided that I didn't want to do that any more. Then things got a little more difficult.

On Monday morning he would pack. Before Bri-Nylon and its ability to dry overnight hanging from the back of some rural bed and breakfast bedside chair he had one shirt and three exchangeable collars. I learned my packing from him. He gave me that. I am an expert packer. In the Ryanair age this is not something to be sneered at.

The battered blue cardboard suitcase contained the shirt, the fully elasticated underpants, two pairs of socks, darning materials for same in the event of heel or toe holes, three pressed hankies, a spare tie and a jumper or cardigan for relaxing in and a tired and frayed sponge-soled pair of beige-brown patterned slippers. The toiletries had the shaving gubbins – blades, razor, brush, stick of shaving soap, one bottle of Old Spice, a jar of Morgan's pomade, two hairbrushes (one to hold the hair down, the other to slurp into rigidity enough to last the day) and a brown plastic tortoiseshell-design comb for the final slicked, seal-like flourish.

He wore his suit and shoes and 'normal' tie. A black polished pair of shoes with steel edges on the sides of the heel he came down most upon. He clacked whilst walking. In winter a grey or brown cardigan underneath the jacket, and an overcoat.

Bob Geldof did this, did that and the other. Then a bit more of that and a little of this as well. Later he did some other stuff. On the way he had some luck and often as not, none. So in the end (wouldn't you know it!) more or less the same as everyone else. And so that was that.

The Most Recent Official Biography of B. Geldof, 2014 [trademark protected]

None of this ever changed.

He travelled the country roads before they were really roads, selling his towels and rugs and sometimes Phoenix crockery to an, I imagine, fairly disinterested clientele. In my mind it was probably lonely but in reality I think he loved it. Nights with the other 'who-do-you-do-fers', the self-styled Knights of the Road. Oh there were some 'right buffs' that he couldn't stand but in general there was the gossip and the camaraderie, such as it might be.

He had his routes. Kilkenny-Kilrush-Killaloe-Killakee. I don't know if that's right or not. It sounds right in my mind. Back then I knew them by rote much as one might know the shipping forecast and its far-off mystery mantra: 'Fairisle-Humber-Fastnet-German Bight...'. German bite! Now there's one for yeh.

And he had his B&Bs and the lonely country nights in the shared rooms with some other barely known traveller to keep the costs down on the extremely tight budget. He said he went for walks. He never talked about going to the pub. But he must have. He knew his food. He had been a chef. He never complained about the stuff he must have been given in those basic days. Or the many lonely meals in the wherever-you-can-get-food-at-this-time-of-night towns. And he always ate whatever he was served. There were no gastropubs or restaurants in Killakee. Wherever that is, if it exists at all.

He never called home. There were no phones. Sometimes – and this now strikes me in the email age as bizarre – he'd write a letter and we'd get it, I assume, the next day, because he'd have been home soon after so it would have been pointless. It never said much. Exhorting us to be good, do our homework. How the weather was in Killakee, etc.

He grew to know all his customers and their families and they in turn looked forward to his visits and I suppose ordered things from him just to give him the work. Eventually he ended up staying above the shop with them and on his death many came to his funeral and those that couldn't wrote or sent flowers. Many were the children and grandchildren of his original clients.

→

My mother had died and he was lonely. Did he have girlfriends around about? I don't know, but he must have. He had been a beautiful man and remained, despite the Y-fronts, stylishly handsome and effortlessly charming. Women loved him.

I know he felt guilty leaving his three children on those Mondays. I felt a great expelling of air. I could breathe again. He felt guilt but he also, I believe, like me, felt relief. I'm sure of it. Free. The atmosphere in the house could be oppressive. My sisters trying to please him and loving him, feeling sad for him, wanting and vying for his attention and then me, the errant, wilfully indifferent boy. Free. Outtathere!!

But how terrible to feel that. How terrible not to be there for his 'poor motherless children'. The delicious luxury of all that guilt (sure what could he do? He had to earn a crust by going away, but still...) as you nosed the Hillman into top, the blue suitcase bumping companionably in the back seat.

Later I knew and loved him for the excellent man he was, but back then, how I dreaded his homecoming those Friday nights. I couldn't help it either. Perhaps he did too. Both of us on duty for forty-eight hours pretending to be the very thing we were not and could never be. Perhaps he knew that it was his house, but it was our home. Not his. He wasn't there. Not that much different to the B&B he'd just vacated, really. Except you sort of knew the guy in the other bed a bit better. Me. He had to pretend that we were a family. That nothing was odd. But it was.

―――――

Sam Dyson
+ his father James Dyson

My dad's father died when he was just nine years old. I've often wondered what that must have been like for him, not to have a role model or that father figure who loves you unconditionally. I'm sure that this loss had a huge impact in shaping who my dad is now, with a steely determination that 'you're in it for yourself' and that 'nobody is going to help you'. His approach to life is that if you want to make something happen, you and only you can do it.

My father writes of the loneliness and emotional bereavement he felt growing up without his dad. I have been incredibly fortunate to have had a very different upbringing. I grew up in an extremely loving family, and I know that both Mum and Dad felt that it was very important for me, my brother Jake and my sister Emily, to grow up in a secure home environment.

The idea for the vacuum cleaner came to my dad around the time I was born. He started developing it in the basement of our home. I was too little, but Jake remembers Dad disappearing into the basement for days on end, sometimes smashing up prototypes in frustration. This must have been a really tough time for him, with a young family to support, painstakingly working on an invention that he knew was possible, desperately trying to make it work, all on his own with no support from anyone but his family. He had an unbelievable amount of belief in what he was doing and some serious determination to persevere. Back in those days, making a prototype or even a single component could take weeks, and when things didn't work, or broke, you'd have to start all over again.

The first five years of my life coincided with the prototype stage, and I remember when I was around six years old he had finally developed the first cyclonic vacuum cleaner, which was pink with a see-through bin. It looked beautiful and unlike anything else on the market. There was a very exciting moment when he managed

→

Sam Dyson, the youngest son of Sir James Dyson, was born in 1978. He is a songwriter and lead guitarist with The Chemists. He has founded his own record company, Distiller Records.

to get a slot on a BBC television programme called *Tomorrow's World*. We used to watch this religiously as a family as it was all about innovation and the latest technology about to come on to the market. It was incredibly exciting to see my dad on TV, and was the first moment when I realized that he was doing something groundbreaking. After this breakthrough, Dad was away a lot, trying to license the product to various companies, and we missed him greatly. This must have been a really tough time for my mum as she was on her own with three children, and must have also required a great deal of belief in my dad.

By this point, Dad had moved his workshop and business into a barn that was next to the house. This was great as he was always nearby and I was able to see at first hand what was involved in developing and manufacturing things. They had a lathe machine, milling machines, all kinds of metals and plastics and I used to get really excited about being able to make things. Dad was always really supportive and would help me in the workshop where it felt like anything was possible.

I loved design and art at school, and once I had left I went to work at Dyson as an engineer for three years. During that time, I experienced a side to my dad that I had never seen before. I remember times in our team when we would be trying to solve a problematic design issue. There would be a weekly design review with my dad, so we would try to resolve the issues prior to those meetings and then the eight or so engineers would pile into his office and present possible solutions. On several occasions I remember my dad looking at what we had done, thinking for a couple of minutes and then saying 'Have you thought about doing it like this?' He'd get his pencil out and sketch an always-superior solution that nobody had considered, leaving the team of engineers very quiet! It always fascinated me how his mind worked on a completely different level like this, and gave me a huge sense of admiration for his design and engineering abilities.

As an adult, I have found our relationship to be tougher and more complicated. Dad has been incredibly successful and I believe that a lot of that stems from him losing his dad at such a young age and having to fight his corner. Running Dyson and always having to be ahead of the competition is a constant battle, which he has now been fighting relentlessly for the past thirty-five years. He has had to deal with some huge, aggressive companies that have continually tried to rip off his ideas, sue him and essentially squash him out of the game. There's an injustice here that has made him fight with that steely determination to the bitter end every time, until he (usually) wins.

We all have our own families now, and there are six grandchildren. Dad is wonderfully playful and caring with the grandchildren, but I think he finds it more difficult to be emotionally open with my brother, sister and me. Sometimes I wish I had the fight in me that Dad does. I am a much softer person and can be far more forgiving, although I do have a core determination to never give up and am becoming more assertive and decisive as I learn more about business and managing people. I now run a record label and publishing company, and am touring a lot with my band, all of which I owe to my parents.

As a family, we continue to develop the business 'in the Dyson way', with the core principles and ethos that my dad instilled in us as well as in his workforce. This is a daunting challenge, and also a source of huge pride. Do we have it in us? I don't know if my dad will ever be able to give up control, but I think he feels a lot of love and satisfaction at the fact that we are prepared to try. There is something really wonderful about standing side by side and working together towards the same goal.

I feel so lucky to have a father who has been and continues to be an inspiration and support to me in so many ways. I look forward to our relationship evolving.

I do try to inspire my own children now, and I repeatedly tell them that anything in life is possible if you absolutely believe in yourself and you work hard to achieve your goals. They have an amazing role model in their grandfather.

Neil Jordan
+ his father Michael Jordan

I have written about my father many times, but always disguised him. The first disguise was in a short story, 'Night in Tunisia', where he became a saxophone player who played in a showband and wanted his son to share his musical tastes. The son, of course, didn't. The next disguise was as a photographer, in a novel, *The Past*, whose son, as far as I remember, had no idea he was his son. There was another disguise in another novel, *Sunrise with Seamonster*, where he became a wheelchair-confined autocrat, married to a piano teacher with whom the son was, of course, in love.

Donal McCann played a piece of my father in a small movie, *The Miracle*, and Patrick McCabe played a version of him in a film I made of his novel *Breakfast on Pluto*. And oddly enough, Patrick's portrayal was the closest to the man in question (he taught Pat in St Patrick's Training College where he was a lecturer…).

The scene we had written had nothing to do with my father, but involved an exasperated schoolteacher dealing with an impossibly imaginative, impossibly feminine boy. Pat, who is only an occasional actor, took so long in costume that I wondered what was going on. Then out he came, wearing a cardigan with leather patches stitched into the sleeves, head bent slightly to one side, a pile of copybooks under his arm, straight into a classroom full of unruly kids who fell immediately into order.

I photographed the scene the way I would have photographed a documentary, watching this extraordinary embodiment of the man I had known, but never really looked at. So if anyone wants to know what he was like, they should watch that scene, from that film. Or look at this portrait that my sister made of him when she was in her late teens. He had softened by then, and she was, I think, his favourite. I can see the affection in this pencil portrait. I can also see the accuracy, which could only be enabled by affection, which makes me think maybe they're the same thing.

Neil Jordan was born in Sligo, Ireland, in 1950. He is a writer and film director. He began his writing career by winning The *Guardian* Fiction Prize for his book of short stories, *Night in Tunisia*, in 1976. Since then he has published five novels. He has written and directed more than twenty films and won an Academy Award for Best Original Screenplay for *The Crying Game* in 1993. He was the instigator and creative force behind the TV series *The Borgias*. He is married and has five children.

Daddy, Asleep by Dervil Jordan
Jordan private collection

Hanif Kureishi
+ his father Rafiushan Kureishi

Something Given

My father wanted to be a writer. I can't remember a time when he didn't want this. There were few mornings when he didn't go to his desk – early, at about six o'clock – in one of his many suits and coloured shirts, the cuffs pinned by bejewelled links, before he left for work carrying his briefcase, longside the other commuters. Writing was, I suppose, an obsession, and as with most obsessions, fulfillment remained out of reach. The obsession kept him incomplete but it kept him going. He had a dull, enervating civil-service job, and writing provided him with something to look forward to. It gave him meaning and 'direction', as he liked to put it. It gave him direction home too, since he wrote often about India, the country he left in his early twenties and to which he never returned.

Many of my dad's friends considered his writing to be a risible pretension, though he had published two books for young people, on the history and geography of Pakistan. But even for my father, who loved seeing his name in print – I remember him labouring over the figures for average rainfalls, and on the textile industry – this was not authentic writing. He wanted to be a novelist.

He did write novels, one after another, on the desk he had had a neighbour build for him in the corner of the bedroom he shared with my mother. He wrote them, and he rewrote them, and he rewrote them. Then he typed them out, making copies with several sheets of carbon paper. Sometimes, when his back hurt, he sat on the floor and wrote, with his spine pressed against the wardrobe. But whatever his posture, every workday morning I would hear his alarm, and soon after he would be hammering at his big typewriter. The sound pounded into us like artillery fire, rocking the house. He wrote at the weekends too, on Sunday afternoons. He would have liked to write in the evenings but by nine o'clock he'd be asleep on the sofa. My mother would wake him, and he'd shuffle off to bed.

In one sense his persistence paid off. By the time he was sixty he must have completed five or six novels, several short stories and a few radio plays. For many writers

Hanif Kureishi was born in London in 1954 to a Pakistani father and an English mother. He is the author of novels including *The Buddha of* *Suburbia* and most recently *The Last Word*; story collections including *Love in a Blue Time*, *Midnight All Day* and *The Body*; plays including *Outskirts* and *Sleep With Me;* and screenplays including *My Beautiful Laundrette* and *Le Week-end*. He was awarded the CBE in 2008.

this would be considered a lifetime's work. Often he became dejected – when he couldn't make a story live; or when he could, but had to break off and leave for the office; or when he was too tired to write; and in particular when his books were turned down by publishers, as all of them were, none of them ever reaching the public. His despair was awful; we all despaired along with him. But any encouragement from a publisher – even a standard letter expressing interest – renewed his vigour. Whether this was folly or dedication depends on your point of view. In the end all he wanted was for someone to say: 'This is brilliant, it moved me. You are a wonderful writer.' He wanted to be respected as he respected certain writers.

Once, in Paris, where I was staying, I went to a restaurant with one of my father's elder brothers. He was one of my favourite uncles, famous for his carousing but also for his violent temper. After a few drinks I admitted to him that I'd come to Paris to write, to learn to be a writer. He subjected me to a tirade of abuse. Who do you think you are, he said, Balzac? You're a fool, he went on, and your father's a fool too, to encourage you in this. It is pretentious, idiotic. Fortunately, I was too young to be discouraged; I knew how to keep my illusions going. But I was shocked by what my father had had to endure from his family. You couldn't get above your station; you couldn't dream too wildly.

Perhaps my uncles and Father's acquaintances found his passion eccentric because Asian people in Britain hadn't uprooted themselves to pursue the notoriously badly paid and indulgent profession of 'artist'. They had come to Britain to make lives for themselves that were impossible at home. At that time, in the mid 1960s, the images of India that we saw on television were of poverty, starvation and illness. In contrast, in the south of Britain, people who had survived the war and the miserable 1950s were busily acquiring fridges, cars, televisions, washing-machines.

For immigrants and their families, disorder and strangeness is the condition of their existence. They want a new life and the material advancement that goes with it. But having been ripped from one world and flung into another, what they also require, to keep everything together, is tradition, habitual ideas, stasis. Life in the country you have left may move on, but life in the diaspora is often held in a strange suspension, as if the act of moving has provided too much disturbance as it is.

Culture and art was for other people, usually wealthy, self-sufficient people who were safe and established. It was naive to think you could be a writer; or it was a kind of showing-off. Few of father's friends read; not all of them were literate. Many of them were recent arrivals, and they worked with him in the Pakistan embassy. In the evening they worked in shops, or as waiters, or in petrol stations. They were sending money to their families. Father would tell me stories of omnivorous aunts and brothers and parents who thought their fortunate benefactor was living in plenty. They knew nothing of the cold and rain and abuse and homesickness. Sometimes they had clubbed together to send their relative to England who would then be obliged to remit money. One day the family would come over to join him. Until this happened the immigrant would try to buy a house; then another. Or a shop, or a factory.

$\rightarrow$

For others, whose families were in Britain, the education of their children was crucial. And this, along with money, was the indicator par excellence of their progress in the new country. And so, bafflingly to me, they would interminably discuss their cars.

Even we had to get a car. Most of the time it sat rusting outside the house, and my sister and I would play in it, since it took Father six attempts to get through the driving test. He became convinced that he was failed because of racial prejudice. Eventually he complained to the Race Relations Board, and next time he passed. Not long after he crashed the car with all of us in it.

Writing was the only thing Father wanted to be interested in, or good at, though he could do other things: cook, be an attentive and entertaining friend, play sports. He liked being a father. His own father, a doctor, had had twelve children, of which ten were sons. My father had never received the attention he required. He felt his life had lost 'direction' due to lack of guidance. He knew, therefore, what a father should be. It wasn't a question for him. He and I would play cricket for hours in the garden and park; we went to the cinema – mostly to watch war films like *Where Eagles Dare*; we watched sport on television, and we talked.

Father went to the library every Saturday morning, usually with me in tow. He planted notebooks around the house – in the toilet, beside his bed, in the front room beside his television chair – in order to write wherever he was. These notebooks he made himself from a square of cardboard and a bulldog clip, attaching to them various odd-shaped sheets of paper – the backs of flyers that came through the letterbox, letters from the bank, paper he took from work, envelopes. He made little notes exhorting himself onwards: 'the whole secret of success is; the way to go is; one must begin by…; this is how to live, to think, to write…'. He would clench his fist and slam it into the palm of his other hand, saying, 'one must fight'.

Father was seriously ill during much of my youth, with a number of painful and depressing ailments. But even in hospital he would have a notebook at hand. When dying he talked of his latest book with his usual touching but often infuriating grandiosity. 'In my latest novel I am showing how a man feels when…' My mother, quite sensibly, wondered whether he might not be better off doing something less frustrating than shutting himself away for most of his spare time. Life was slipping away; he wasn't getting anywhere. Did he have to prefer failure as a writer to success at anything else? Perhaps she and he could do things together. Nothing changed, that was the problem. The continuous disappointment that accompanied this private work was hard for everyone to bear, and it was the atmosphere in which we lived. Sometimes Mother suggested the illnesses were precipitated by his hopeless desire for the unattainable. But this was not something Father liked to hear.

He was convinced that she didn't understand what such a passion entailed. The fact was, she did. Yet he wanted to get to people. He had something to say and wanted response. He required attention. The publishers who rejected his work were standing between him and the audience he was convinced was waiting.

Father was good company – funny, talkative, curious, nosy and gossipy. He was always on the lookout for stories. We would work out the plots together. Recently I found one of his stories, which concerns the Indian servant of an English couple living in Madras before the Second World War. The story soon makes it clear that the servant is having an affair with his mistress. Towards the end we learn that he is also having an affair with the master. If I was surprised by this fertile story of bisexuality, I always knew he had an instinct for ironies, links, parallels, twists.

He liked other people and would talk with the neighbours as they dug their gardens and washed their cars, and while they stood together on the station in the morning. He would give them nicknames and speculate about their lives until I couldn't tell the difference between what he'd heard and what he'd imagined he'd heard. 'Suppose, one day,' he'd say, 'that man over there decided to…' And off he would go. As Maupassant wrote, 'You can never feel comfortable with a novelist, never be sure that he will not put you into bed one day, quite naked, between the pages of a book.'

It amused Father, and amazed me – it seemed like a kind of magic – to see how experience could be converted into stories, and how the monotony and dullness of an ordinary day could contain meaning, symbolism and even beauty. The invention and telling of stories – that most indispensable human transaction – brought us together. There was amusement, contact, entertainment. Whether this act of conversion engaged Father more closely with life, or whether it provided a necessary distance, or both, I don't know. Nevertheless, Father understood that in the suburbs, where concealment is often the only art, but where there is so much aspiration, dreaming and disappointment – as John Cheever illustrated – there is a lot for a writer.

Perhaps after a certain age Father couldn't progress. Yet he remained faithful to this idea of writing. It was his religion, his reason for living, the God he couldn't betray and the God who wouldn't let him down. Father's art involved a long fidelity and a great commitment. Like many lives in the suburbs, it was also a long deferral. One day in the future – when his work was published and he was recognized as a writer – good things would happen to him and everything would change. But for the time being everything remained the same. He was fixed, and, from a certain point of view, stuck. Yet father would not stop writing. It was crucial to him that these stories be told. Like Scheherazade, he was writing for his life.

I started to write seriously around the age of fourteen or fifteen. At school I felt that what I was expected to learn was irrelevant and tedious. The teachers didn't conceal their boredom. Like us, they couldn't wait to get out. I felt I was being stuffed with the unwanted by fools. I couldn't make the information part of myself; it had to be held at a distance, like unpleasant food. The alternative was compliance. Or there was rebellion.

Then there was writing, which was an active way of taking possession of the world. I could be omnipotent, rather than a victim. Writing became a way of processing, ordering, what seemed like chaos. If I wrote because my father did, I soon learned that writing was the

→

one place where I had dominion, where I was in charge. At a desk in my study, enwombed, warm, concentrated, self-contained, with everything I needed to hand – music, pens, paper, typewriter – I could make a world in which disharmonies could be contained, and perhaps drained of their poison. I wrote to make myself feel better, because often I didn't feel too good. I wrote to become a writer and get away from the suburbs. But while I was there my father's storytelling enlivened the half-dead world for me.

I remember some of my father's friends complaining to him about my work, particularly *My Beautiful Laundrette*. For Asians in the west, or for anyone in exile, intellectual and emotional disarray can seem unbearable. The artist may be a conduit for the forbidden, for that which is too dangerous to say, but he isn't always going to be thanked for his trouble.

I wrote, too, because it was absorbing. I was fascinated by how one thing led to another. Once I'd started banging on my typewriter, in my bedroom above Father's, I wanted to see what might be done, where such creative curiosity might lead me. You'd be in the middle of a story, in some unfamiliar imaginative place, but you'd only got there because you'd been brave enough to start off. I was impatient, which hindered me. As soon as I began something I wanted to get to the end of it. I want to succeed rather than search. I wanted to be the sort of person who had written books, rather than a person who was merely writing them. Probably I inherited father's desperation as a kind of impatience. I am still impatient; it isn't much fun sitting at a desk with nothing happening. But at least I can see the necessity for impatience in writing – the desire to have something done, which must push against the necessity to wait, for the rumination that allows you to see how a piece of writing might develop or need to find its own way over time, without being hurried to a conclusion.

I conceived the idea of what became *The Buddha of Suburbia* on the balcony of a hotel room in Madras, my father's birthplace. Until then, as a professional writer, I had written plays and films, though I'd already published the first chapter of *The Buddha of Suburbia* as a short story. Ever since it had appeared in print the characters and situation remained with me. Normally you finish something with a sense of relief. It is over because you are bored with it and, for now – until the next time – you have said as much as you can. But I had hardly begun. I knew – my excitement told me – that I had material for a whole book: south London in the 1970s, growing up as a 'semi-Asian' kid; pop, fashion, drugs, sexuality. My task was to find a way to organize it.

When my films were made and books published Father was delighted, if not a little surprised. It was what he wanted, except that it happened to me rather than to him. Towards the end of his life, which coincided with my becoming a professional writer, he became more frantic. He left his job, wrote more, and sent his books around the publishing houses with increasing desperation. At times he blamed me for his failure to get published. Surely I could help him as he had helped me? Even as he took pride in what I was doing, my success was mocking him. For the first time he seemed to have become bitter. If I could do it, why couldn't he? Why can some people tell jokes, do imitations, juggle with knives and balance plates on their nose, while others can only make soufflés? How is it that people might persist in wanting to do something they will never excel at? Is writing difficult?

Only if you can't do it.

I like to work every day, in the morning, like my father. That way I am faithful to him and to myself. I miss it badly if I don't do it. It has become a habit but it is not only that. It gives the day a necessary weight. I'm never bored by what I do. I go to it now with more rather than less enthusiasm. There is less time, of course, while there is more to say about the process of time itself. There are more characters, more experience and numerous ways of approaching it. If writing were not difficult it wouldn't be enjoyable. If it is too easy you might feel you haven't quite grasped the story, that you have omitted something essential. But the difficulty is more likely to be internal to the work itself – where it should be – rather than in some personal crisis. I'm not sure you become more fluent as you get older, but you become less fearful of imagined consequences. There has been a lot to clear away; then the work starts.

———

Bobby Shriver
+ his father Sargent Shriver

In 1969, I was arrested for smoking marijuana. Robert Kennedy had been murdered in June, 1968. Edward Kennedy was the likely Democratic Party presidential nominee for 1972. His nephew being arrested for 'drugs' was a national story. And not a good one.

Various family members were upset (if this were not a family book, I might use a different word). The mood in our Hyannisport house reflected that emotion. Hundreds of reporters and police officers hovered outside the door. Distraught family members monitored the barber as my cousin Bobby Kennedy and I had our hair trimmed.

Into that walked my father. The news had reached him in France. He came to Cape Cod immediately. I did not know what to expect. We went to my room. He closed the door. 'You're a good kid,' he said as soon as I was seated. 'This is a lot of crap. I'm going to take care of it and take you to California. Don't worry.'

I did not say one word.

He made that happen. Two days later, a judge released us to our parents' custody. We went to California.

Fathering children means this much. And no doubt a lot more. To know when your vulnerable son needs to see, and feel, manliness. Many moments of other forms of manliness (playing brutal tennis or football) arose in my life with him, but this one shines through as extreme toughness… in all its wisdom and mercy.

Robert Sargent Shriver III was born in Chicago in 1954 to Sargent Shriver and Eunice Kennedy Shriver, the first of their five children. He is an activist, attorney, journalist and politician living in Santa Monica, California. He has long been associated with the Special Olympics, founded by his mother in 1968, and has worked as a producer on films including *True Lies*. In 2002 he co-founded **DATA** (Debt, Aids, Trade in Africa, now called ONE.org) with Bono of U2. This led to co-founding Product (Red), a brand-licensing company to raise money for the Global Fund, which has raised many millions. He is married to Malissa Feruzzi and they have two daughters.

Bobby Shriver and his father Sargent Shriver
Shriver private collection

Colum McCann
+ his father Sean McCann

My father was, or rather is, a rosarian. For decades he has raised and bred roses in the back garden of our suburban home on Clonkeen Road in Dublin. He spent much of his time in a small greenhouse, puttering about with seedlings and soil and secateurs. It was, for him, a laboratory for joy. In the winter he dragged a kerosene heater to the greenhouse. In summer he opened the glass panels wide and let the breeze in.

Every day he walked down the lawn, in his flat hat and gloves and his Garden News jacket, absorbed and intent. The jacket was ripped asunder by thorns so that the inner lining hung out.

Sometimes he looked to me like the first man ever to whistle.

We had about seven hundred roses in our small garden. Miniatures, hybrid teas, floribundas, climbers. My father talked to his roses – actually talked to them. He was adamant that the ones he talked to grew better, with strong colour, good foliage, hardiness. If they took, he would name them. So many things in this world refuse naming, but not my father's roses: Sally Mac (named for my mother), Bloomsday (for James Joyce), Isabella (for my daughter), Loretta's Rose (for Loretta Brennan Glucksman), Kiss 'n' Tell (for life itself), and Brightness (for a novel I wrote).

In summertime the garden blazed with colour. In winter he went out and pruned the roses back so the garden was kept young and fit and stark.

I have always admired my father immensely, but I disliked working with the roses. I didn't mix the potting soil. I never learned how to breed the seeds. Occasionally I ran the lawnmower, but that was about it.

Twice a year, huge piles of manure arrived from the local farms for my brothers to fertilize the ground. Once my pitchfork revealed a tiny baby calf. The contours of the world were complicated: even the garden was brought to life by death.

Colum McCann was born in Dublin in 1965. He is the author of six novels and two collections of stories. He has won many international literary awards including the 2009 National Book Award and the 2010 Dublin Impac Prize. His work has been published in more than thirty-five languages and he was nominated for an Oscar for his short film, *Everything in this Country Must*, in 2005. He lives in New York where he teaches at Hunter College.

My father was at ease in his garden. The work was in compliance with beauty. The rest of the world – his job in a national newspaper, the pressures of raising a large family, the economics of the times – seemed to disappear, and often when I looked out the kitchen window to search for him I could not see him. He was most likely bent down to one of his seedlings, or dumping the new-mown grass at the bottom of the hedges, or in the rear shed preparing the spray for the greenfly – there were so many tasks to a simple hobby – but in later years it struck me that really he had become part of the landscape, of it and in it.

Once, in the early 1970s, when my sister answered the door, there was a man on our doorstep asking for our father. She said he was busy. The man insisted. He was there to collect a payment, or make a demand of some sort. Where was my father? he asked again. My sister, before gently closing the door, said again that he was busy. But busy where? said the man with his foot in the door. He was, said my sister, down in the back garden, 'playing God'.

Although he can't work the garden any more, my father, in his mid eighties, is still sharp and incisive. Most of the roses are gone, ploughed up, replaced by lawn and patio tiles, but there are still a few bushes around, in pots at the back of the house, in flowerbeds, and every now and then he likes to take his wheelchair into the back garden and wander down amongst them, taking joy in their presence.

He can still be seen talking to them, but I have no idea what it is that he says as he leans over. Nor, frankly, do I want to know. Sometimes, I suppose, we have to allow a little mystery to grow around our fathers.

———

Paul Muldoon
for a son

Some Pitfalls and How to Avoid Them

Stratocumulus, or *cumulonimbus*, the clouds have made such strides
in crossing the Rockies
they've now caught up with us. A diet of buffalo ragout
will leave anyone 'in straits'

sooner rather than later. That the glister in a Port-A-John
on a parking lot near Bennigan's
in Fargo, North Dakota, turned out to be a pine cone
doesn't mean the Cheyenne

were wrong to take things at face value.
Bear in mind that 'calomel' looks a lot like 'chamomile'
to the guy trying to compile
a camping checklist. Given the near certainty they'll fall foul

of some infection of the blood,
snake-bite, sundry blisters and boils,

syphilis, dysentery, piles
and plain old costiveness, Lewis and Clark plied

Paul Muldoon was born in 1951 in County Armagh, Northern Ireland, and educated in Armagh and at Queen's University Belfast. From 1973 to 1986 he worked for the BBC in Belfast as a radio and television producer. Since 1987 he has lived in the United States, where he is now Howard G.B. Clark '21 University Professor in the Humanities at Princeton. Between 1999 and 2004 he was Professor of Poetry at Oxford. Paul Muldoon's main collections of poetry are *New Weather* (1973), *Mules* (1977), *Why Brownlee Left* (1980), *Quoof* (1983), *Meeting The British* (1987), *Madoc: A Mystery* (1990), *The Annals of Chile* (1994), *Hay* (1998), *Poems 1968-1998* (2001) and *Moy Sand and Gravel* (2002), for which he won the 2003 Pulitzer Prize. He is poetry editor of *The New Yorker*.

their entire squad
with Dr Rush's Bilious Pills,
the upshot being the Corps of Discovery would loosen their bowels
by thunderclaps and quicksilver-scoots

through random pine scrub and clumps of river birch.
Now we've pulled into the Samurai
Sushi Bar and ordered two Godzilla rolls. Bear in mind that Zimri
was King of Israel only as long as it took to purge

himself of himself. Who would have guessed
that J.M.W. Turner was perfecting his ability to scumble
cumulonimbus and *stratocumulus*
precisely as Lewis and Clark reached the Pacific coast

and built Fort Clatsop? The Cheyenne chewed the gum
of both ponderosa
and lodgepole pines. Bear in mind how our fireside banter
may be lost to the generations to come

but their native scouts
will still be able to follow our route across America
by the traces of mercury
in our scats.

———

John Julius Norwich
+ his father Duff Cooper

When my father died – on New Year's Day 1954, in mid Atlantic – he was sixty-three and I was twenty-four. Two years earlier I had married and joined the Foreign Service; but I had been a lamentably slow developer, and though he and I loved each other dearly I never felt that I was much fun for him. If he had lived to my present age of eighty-four, I should have discovered my fascination with history and we should long ago have conquered that slight shyness that always existed between us. He would, I hope, have enjoyed my books – he would certainly have been much happier to have a writer, rather than a diplomat, as a son – and I should have benefited enormously from his help and advice.

As things turned out, he inevitably tended to take a back seat behind my mother. For one thing, she had far more leisure. He, first as a highly conscientious member of parliament and subsequently as a cabinet minister, had neither the time nor, very probably, the inclination for too much of my infant company; my mother on the other hand saw me as something not far short of a full-time job, starting me off on reading, arithmetic and geography when I was three, taking me to the museums and the zoo and performances of Shakespeare, or sometimes just getting into her car and chasing fire engines. My father simply couldn't compete. But in those pre-television evenings and on weekends he loved reading aloud to us – there was not a nineteenth- or early twentieth-century novel in English or French that he hadn't read and remembered – and I always knew that family life was important to him.

This, however, did not mean marital fidelity. For virtually all his adult life he was never without a mistress – sometimes three or four. He made no secret of the fact, least of all to my mother, who minded only when she believed the lady concerned to be unworthy of him. Normally, they tended to become close friends. One of them, the

---

John Julius Norwich was born in 1929. After an education at Upper Canada College in Toronto, Eton, the University of Strasbourg and Oxford, he spent twelve years in the Foreign Service before resigning to become a writer. He has written histories of Norman Sicily, Venice, the Byzantine Empire, the Mediterranean and the Papacy, travel books on Mount Athos and the Sahara, and others on music and architecture. He has also made some thirty historical documentaries for BBC Television and has appeared regularly on the radio programmes *My Word* and *Round Britain Quiz*. His recreation is nightclub piano.

French poetess Louise de Vilmorin, actually spent weeks living in the Paris embassy during his tenure; I remember how she and my mother and myself, then about sixteen, once went on a week's tour of the Pyrenees while my father remained in the office. After his death she and another of his favourites – Susan Mary Alsop, who actually went so far as to present me with a half-brother – always stayed with my mother whenever they came to London. Years later, I asked her if she had really never minded. 'Not a bit,' she said, 'why should I mind if they made him happy? Besides, I always knew: they were the flowers, I was the tree.' It was true: again and again in his diaries he writes of some lady or other, 'but of course she's nothing compared with Diana' or 'but if I had to choose between her and Diana it would be like choosing between night and day.' What did I, a teenager, think of all this? As I remember, I assumed – if indeed I thought at all – that all these relationships were perfectly innocent. I was certainly in no way surprised or shocked, but there: as I said, I was a slow developer.

Certainly, the huge admiration that I always felt for my father remained unaffected. It was not just that he had a marvellous sense of humour and was tremendous fun; I loved his passion for books, and above all for poetry: he could recite for hours and was no mean poet himself. (One of his parlour tricks was to dictate a sonnet, composing it as he went along.) And I was always intensely proud of him – in particular of his courage, both physical and moral. I would boast to my school-friends of how, in August 1918, he had won the D.S.O. by attacking a German machine-gun nest single-handed and returning with eighteen prisoners; and I myself remembered how twenty years later he was the only minister in Neville Chamberlain's cabinet to have resigned – as First Lord of the Admiralty, a job he loved as much as any that he ever held – over the Munich agreement with Hitler.

He was, I think, one of the happiest men I ever knew. With the single exception of music – to which he was tone deaf, unable to identify the national anthem until other people stood up – he loved all the pleasures of life and enjoyed them to

→

the full; nothing, I suspect – not even women – gave him more pleasure than the company of his friends round a table well stocked with food and drink. And these, finally, were his undoing. By the time he reached the embassy his liver had taken a considerable battering; the last thing it needed was a regime of two immense French meals every day – and this was a time when lunch as well as dinner tended to begin with two pulverizing dry martinis. But he was in no sense an alcoholic. The only time I ever saw him drunk was when he returned from an 'intimate dinner' with the Soviet ambassador. He had lost count of the toasts after the first fifteen, was confined to bed for a fortnight and never touched vodka again.

Nor did he ever properly recover his health. For the last three or four years of his life he ate relatively little and drank nothing stronger than ginger ale. And it was now, I feel reasonably sure, that he showed the greatest courage of all: knowing full well that he was dying of cirrhosis, he never divulged the fact to my mother or to me. The only hint he gave was in the last sentence of his autobiography, *Old Men Forget*, completed months before his death. 'Autumn has always been my favourite season,' he wrote, 'and evening has been for me the pleasantest time of day. I love the sunlight but I cannot fear the coming of the dark.'

———

Adam Clayton
+ his father Brian Clayton

When I think back over the interactions between my father and me there are very few moments to which I return and say, 'That was pivotal to how things turned out.' My father is a practical man; he is not naturally affected by music or art and I think believes that getting in touch with his feminine side was listening to my mother.

In 1974 I had persuaded my mother to buy me a budget bass guitar, which she did with the proviso that I had to learn to play it – by 1976 I hadn't mastered it but had identified that I needed a better instrument in order to learn and my father was essential to this plan.

He flew regularly to New York and second-hand instruments were much cheaper at Manny's of 48th Street. This was a long time before the internet and required my father to walk into the inhospitable domain of a music shop in New York filled with hipsters and hippies making as much noise as possible to attract attention. I had given him the arguments that a used bass would cost 125 dollars in the US, half of what it would cost at home, and I could probably sell my old bass for sixty pounds so I would be ahead with the new investment. He agreed and I gave him the money and the magic words 'Fender Precision bass' – and waited.

The day came when the bass arrived with him from New York. It was a Sunburst finish and smelt and handled differently than anything else I had experienced. I felt like a Beatle, a Rolling Stone, a Strangler, a Clash man. I often have this same feeling when touching an instrument for the first time – a recollection that goes back to the moment I first opened that case from New York.

I doubt my father has a similar recall but I often think of what it was like for him to enter that music shop, and armed with only a little information, engage with a salesman and hope to be treated fairly and respectfully. I wonder how it was for him to carry it back to Dublin explaining to work colleagues that it was an electric bass for his son Adam, 'who couldn't really play it'.

Adam Clayton was born in 1960 in Oxfordshire, England. His father was an RAF pilot and then worked in civil aviation. In 1965 the family moved to Ireland, where he met Bono, The Edge and Larry Mullen Junior at Mount Temple Comprehensive School and together they founded U2 in 1976. As part of the hugely successful group, Clayton has won twenty-two Grammy Awards. He is married to Marianna Teixeira de Carvalho.

Jeff Koons
+ his father Henry Koons

My father was an amazing man. I never met anyone who had known my father who didn't say that he was the nicest person that they had ever met. My dad was completely supportive, generous and optimistic; he was always able to look on the bright side of things and never had any aspect of anger in his being. I remember how calm and patient he was: when we went fishing and I needed my bait changed or a line untangled, my dad would always be attentive and never got overwhelmed. He was like this in all aspects of life.

As far as my involvement in art, my father was always very supportive. I learned aesthetics from my dad. I also learned from him that if you have a vision, you can create it. I would watch my father, an interior decorator, at work. He would start with a piece of graph paper and do an overview of a room and then an elevation drawing. Everything was planned out in advance so that nothing was left to chance and you knew exactly what the final design would look like. So my father showed me how to go about exercising your vision. He taught me how colours and textures can affect the way you feel. I learned from him how emotions and feelings are conveyed through aesthetics.

My father always created situations for our family so that we felt a sense of social mobility. He made sure that we did exciting things. We went on interesting vacations and had experiences that made us feel engaged in the world. He made sure that we could have as broad and interesting a life as possible. We experienced great things as a family.

Some of the fondest memories I have with my father are when I was learning how to swim, being with him in the ocean, fishing with him and working with him at his furniture store on the weekends. I just really enjoyed being in his presence. I'm very grateful for his love and the foundation that he provided for me in life.

I lost my father in 1994. I miss him every day.

Michael Jackson and Bubbles by Jeff Koons,
with Henry and Jeff Koons in foreground
Koons private collection

Jeff Koons was born in 1955. An internationally recognized artist, he is well known for his public sculptures such as the large-scale floral sculpture, *Puppy*. Combining objects from the everyday while at the same time referencing art history, his work revolves around themes of self-acceptance, transcendence and optimism. Typically working in series, Koons' art holds up a mirror to contemporary consumer culture, using the photorealistic, commercial aesthetic familiar from an earlier generation of Pop artists to generate his unique and universally recognizable style. His work has been exhibited extensively around the world and is part of major private and public collections, such as the Whitney Museum of American Art, The Museum of Modern Art in New York City and The Tate Gallery in London. Koons lives and works in New York City.

Perry Ogden
+ his father John Ogden

'Major Square' – that's what my brother and I used to call my father when he wouldn't let us do what we wanted. 'Daddy can we go to the cinema, Daddy can I have money to buy a pair of Dr Martens, Daddy can you buy us a pony?' 'No, no and no,' my father would reply. 'Major Square! Major Square!' we would chant in unison.

My father had run away from school to join the army. His heroes had been military men, men of empire. He had quickly risen through the ranks to major and no doubt had his heart set on a life in the army, but my mother, a journalist, soon tired of army life and wanted to get back to work. My father entered the world of advertising and his office in Berkeley Square soon became a regular stop-off point for me on my way home from school – either to raid the Cadbury's cupboard, pick up some Guinness posters or, even better, get some cash from my dad or his secretary.

It was at his office that my father received a call from my mother about the family car, a Renault 4 – a car that caused many a row between my parents. On this occasion it had broken down on the King's Road. My mother called in a fury to tell my father that she had had enough and had given the key to a passer-by. My father rushed from his office to the King's Road where he found the car – and a man looking somewhat bemused, who gave the key to him.

And then one Monday morning, when I was eleven, I was coming down the stairs from my bedroom to get some breakfast before catching the bus to school. My father appeared on the landing outside his bedroom door, with tears rolling down his cheeks. 'Mummy's died,' he said. How? We had only seen her the day before. We had been to visit her in Westminster Hospital. She had been sitting up in her hospital bed, a big smile on her face. She had given me a shirt with big round collars – a shirt I loved. We were waiting for her to come home.

Perry Ogden was born in 1961 in Shropshire, England, grew up in London and now lives in Dublin. His photographs have appeared in magazines including Italian *Vogue*, *W*, *The New Yorker*, *The Face* and *Arena*, and he has shot advertising campaigns for Ralph Lauren, Chloe and Calvin Klein. These have supplemented more personal projects including the Pony Kids photographs, published by Jonathan Cape/Aperture in 1999. His first film, *Pavee Lackeen* (The Traveller Girl) (2005), won numerous awards. Recent exhibitions include 'Inspiration' at the Sebastian Guinness Gallery in Dublin in 2010 and 'Twenty' at the Irish Museum of Modern Art in 2011.

John Ogden with his sons Perry and William
Ogden private collection

140

→

My mother was Catholic and my father was Anglican. As a young child I was an altar boy at Westminster Cathedral. After my mother died my father continued to take us to the local Catholic church, St Peter and St Paul on Amwell Street. My brother and I would do everything we could to avoid going to church. A favourite trick was to swirl hot water around in our mouths, say we were feeling ill and insist that our temperature be taken. It never really worked.

My father always wanted the best for me. After my mother died he became concerned about the company I was keeping and the cockney accent I was picking up. Football was my obsession and I played whenever I could with my friends from the local flats. So the decision was made to send me away to school. For a short time I went to a prep school in Buckinghamshire where I took the entrance exam for Eton. I discovered many years later that my father sold some family heirlooms to pay the school fees.

Towards the end of my time at Eton a group of us were caught drinking in a pub in Windsor. I was summoned to the Head Master. Armed with a cane, he told me to bend over the beating block and proceeded to give me six – or maybe eight – of the best. It left welts on my backside. On hearing about this my father paid the Head Master a visit, to question whether he should be beating boys.

My father wasn't thrilled when I told him I wanted to be a photographer and he did what he could to try and steer me off this course. Whilst I was working as an apprentice he took my boss out to lunch. He wanted to know what kind of future there was in photography as a career and was told: 'Too late. He's gone.'

But once I was on the path my father was always supportive and took a keen interest in my work. As I've grown older I realize how alike we are in some ways – we both like giving orders! – even though our lives have moved in radically different directions.

My father's eighty now and long retired from advertising. He devotes his time to writing, walking tours and his garden. When we were looking through a copy of his first novel, *On Fire*, published in 2007, about a young British officer in the Korean War, my daughter Violet, who was twenty at the time, asked him when he had started writing the book. 'When I was your age,' my father replied.

My father has lost two wives to cancer. Now he has a girlfriend with a beautiful bottom, Venus Italica. He keeps her in his garden. She puts a smile on his face.

―――――

John Ogden's garden
Ogden private collection

143

Michael Zilkha
+ his father Selim Zilkha

Life is Not a Dress Rehearsal

That's what my father says. And that's how he has lived his life. He ploughs on, no matter the obstacles. Born a Sephardic Jew in Baghdad in 1927, by the age of seventeen he had lived in Lebanon, Egypt (boarding at the English School in Cairo at seven where he learned the language) and was an American college graduate (Williams) and in the US army. He became a banker because that was the family business and one went to work for one's father. My grandfather never learned English so they communicated in Arabic and French, but my father and his brothers and sisters assimilated as they spread out around the globe. That's a necessity for refugees. My father was posted in London. A few years after his father died my father shifted to retailing because he did not enjoy lending money. He and his partner Jimmy Goldsmith bought a chain of chemists from a friend he bumped into at a nightclub in London, and it eventually metamorphosed into Mothercare. My father married his first cousin (my mother) when he was twenty-six and she was seventeen. It didn't work out but then he met Mary and they have been together over fifty years. He doesn't like to make the same mistake twice, so they have never married.

I experienced my father as a monolith growing up. It came from his certainty. He wasn't weak. When I cried at the lunch table he would pick me up and hold me over the plants saying we mustn't let those tears go to waste. And they would dry up. The happiest times with him were when he was building his business. We would set out at 5.30 am on a Saturday to be in Newcastle by the time a shop opened there and then slowly wend our way home. Retail is detail was another of his sayings. And indeed it was. Dinner came replete with new merchandise to test, he knew his manageresses on a first-name basis and retail giants from America would come to

Michael Zilkha was born in 1954 and lives in Houston, Texas. He studied philosophy and French literature at Oxford and then took the first boat to New York City in the summer of 1975.

His first job was reviewing plays at *The Village Voice.* It took Michael three days to discover CBGBs. His career since then is described in his essay. Michael loves fiction, kayaking and spending

time in Maine with his wife, two children and granddaughter. He still looks forward to Tuesdays because that's when the new records come out.

marvel at the way he used his IBM 360 to alert manufacturers about sales and when they should drop-ship merchandise directly to the stores. My father had figured out that central warehouses were unnecessary in a country the size of England. Sunday nights, after golf, he would sit and read stock print outs on every item in the store before we watched *Laugh In* as a family. Backgammon and bridge were the principal outlets for relaxation, and by watching him I became a good backgammon player. Life was an easy set of negotiations. If my sister Nadia and I walked around the golf course, then he would take us to Brian Epstein's Saville Theatre where he would question Eric Clapton's role in Cream because he leaned against his amplifier for most of the set while Jack Bruce and Ginger Baker so obviously exerted themselves.

My father enjoys the journey but not the arrival. And by the time I had finished university Mothercare was public and he had disengaged. The impulsivity that had led him to enter retailing at a time when he had been quoted as saying that the only shops he went into were his tailor's and his shoemaker's had led him in other directions. So I did not go to work for him, and we never even discussed it. This was 1975 and we were no longer so close. I crossed the ocean and after a few years in journalism set out on my own in a business that was far removed from his. With encouragement from another mentor, Chris Blackwell, I started a record company, Ze Records, and developed a fusion of punk music and disco at the time when the two were apart and polarized. I did however continue to measure myself against my father, and despite substantial sales (eventually), and an unimpeachable coolness, this felt to me like little more than a *succès d'estime*. So when my father moved to Los Angeles and made a disastrous investment in an energy company, it was an opportunity to recalibrate the relationship. By building a business from scratch together I might make myself indispensable. I moved to Houston, we found a great CEO and finally started working together. Eleven years later we were the largest acreage owners in shallow waters in the Gulf of Mexico thanks to increased computing power and technology, which enabled us to pinpoint overlooked oil and gas deposits, securing the acreage before others appreciated what was there. We drilled our wells 100 per cent, which went against received wisdom for independents but all the benefits inured to us.

$\rightarrow$

Michael Zilkha

Three generations of Zilkhas:
Michael, Selim and Daniel

We sold our business in early 1998 since competitors had started to copy us. We immediately went into the wind energy business because my father was interested in renewables and a friend had told me that he had read in *Scientific American* that if one blanketed Arizona with wind farms one could power the USA (a very obvious fallacy) … I have never managed to acquire my father's certitude and ability to never look back, but I was no longer the junior partner.

There have been several rifts in our family between fathers and sons who worked together. Yet our second business too was a success, and slowly the relationship equalized. Our third excursion is in process now, seven years without revenue but a possibility to displace huge quantities of coal with a waterproof wood pellet. My father never doubts the outcome. When I become concerned he asks me whether we have a superior product and I answer in the affirmative. Then, he says, it will work. For him, the journey is still more exciting than the arrival.

I become oppressed by the pressure and the commitments we have to make but he calms me down, and with perseverance it might indeed work out. Now my son has joined us straight out of college. Daniel is an amalgam of the two of us. He and my father love discussing sports and playing games, their aspirations and happiness much clearer than mine. Perhaps my father passed his genes onto my son and I was the vessel. Friends of my father's say how similar my father and I are. They will hear me laugh and think it's him. But I know it's not that simple. I enjoy the connection that work provides us, going on trips, just the two of us; I respect the clarity of his judgments, the way he cares, that he has such a distinct sense of right and wrong. But deep down my father is sunnier than I am, with a complete absence of doubt and melancholy. As long as he's occupied – whether discussing business, seeing a film, reading or playing bridge on the computer, or giving parties with Mary – he is happy. Daniel falls somewhere between the two of us on that spectrum. I hope that our three generations will work together for many years, and that my son will learn from us and teach us both. That's the way it's meant to be in Sephardic merchant families.

———

Larry Mullen Jnr
+ his father Laurence Mullen Snr

Of all the requests that I have been tasked with over the years I have to admit that writing something about my dad has been one of the most challenging. It's not that I don't have a lot to say about him. On the contrary, I have endless stories to tell about his little quirks and his sad, funny moments.

No.

It's just that as the lines begin to take shape I can't help thinking that this entry is beginning to read more like an obituary than anything I had planned. For a start my dad is very much alive and in his ninety-first year. We have known each other a long time and I am not sure I could ever do him justice no matter how many words or paragraphs I try to write. Anyhow, I know he could write a far better piece about himself than I ever could. He still has a way with words. I still play the drums.

It's just over ten years since I bought my dad his first laptop – it took a few goes before he mastered it. He sends me regular emails filled with revealing, funny and often touching messages that usually include solid advice and the occasional well-intended blow to the solar plexus.

Shortly after our appearance at the 2014 Golden Globe awards I received the enclosed email from Dad. It was in response to a brief acceptance speech by myself alongside the rest of the band for Best Original Song for 'Ordinary Love' in which I referred to Nelson Mandela's historical contribution to the Irish peace process. Laurence Snr obviously thought this was a stretch:

Larry Mullen Jnr was born in Artane, Dublin, in 1961. He founded rock band U2 by posting a notice on the Mount Temple Comprehensive School noticeboard in 1976 and has been the drummer for the band ever since. His incredibly successful work as a musician paved the way for his acting career. To date he has appeared in three films including *A Thousand Times Goodnight,* which won the Grand Prix at the Montreal Film Festival in 2013. He and his partner Ann Acheson have three children.

From: Laurence Mullen Snr
Subject: Globe Awards
Date: 14 January 2014 19:16:30 GMT+1
To: LaurenceMullenJr

Hi,

Slowly getting used to being in my 90th year, not helped by the miserable cold rainy weather every day in January. I've amassed a good number of cards. I sacrificed looking at other television shows to see a late showing of the Globe awards. Much of it over my head, and not helped by the slobbering acceptance speeches. At least that cannot be said of the contributions from the members of U2. In your case, the reasons for Mandela's visit to Ireland wasn't to solve the IRA/British impasse but **(a)** to thank the Dunnes store staff for their import ban on South African goods and especially fruit and **(b)** to meet Gerry Adams, with whom he had close contacts in his earlier policy of an armed struggle with South African government. Gerry was an honoured guest of the SA government during the prolonged burial ceremonies for Mandela, including being one of the few dignitaries allowed to be present at his actual burial. Well anyway, enough about that.

Hope you are keeping well and finding the new regime to your liking. You all looked good and happy on the tele last night.

Maybe you'd make contact whenever you're free.

Love,

Dad

Acknowledgments

Editor
Kathy Gilfillan

Project Team
Bono, Sebastian Clayton, Marie Donnelly,
Colm A. McDonnell, Ciarán ÓGaora, Colm Tóibín

Design
Zero-G

Copy Editor
Djinn von Noorden

Agent
Ed Victor

Sponsors
Ardagh Group, Park Hyatt Hotel Group, Zero-G

Thanks To
Aimee Bell, Stuart Bell, Aileen Blackwell, Anna Biles, This Brunner, Tracy Bufferd, Gabriel Byrne, Andy Caffrey, Leo Chapman, Olivia Cole, Sadie Coles, Moya and Paul Coulson, Patrick Cousins, Liz Devlin, John Donnelly, Jed Donnelly, Miriam Donohoe, Andrew Emerson, Claudine Farrell, Sinéad Foley, Catriona Garde, Dan Gilmore, Jenny Mushkin Goldman, Loretta Brennan Glucksman, Nathalie Hallam, Mary Harney, Ronan Harris, Ali Hewson, Susan Hunter, Barbara Jakobson, Dylan Jones, Melanie Jones, Paul McCarthy, Gary McGraw, Alexandra McGuinness, Yvonne McGuinness, Debbie McNally, Vanessa Manko, Lara Marlowe, Lucy Matthews, Max von Massenbach, Katherine Melchior-Ray, Sam Merry, Rebecca Miller, Andrew Weld Moore, Giorgio Pace, Amanda Perlyn, Kathryn Phelan, Maggie Phillips, Diana Picasso, Nicholas J. Pritzker, Tom Pritzker, Brenda Rawn, Hannah Richert, Steven Rinehart, Jessie Fortune Ryan, Susan Sandon, Bill Shipsey, John Silberman, Francesca Schwarzenbach, Sonia Thornton, Matthew Turner, Lisa Power, Niall and Fiona Wall, Anna-Sophia Watts, Marie Weston, Helen Williams, Pippa Wright, Jason Ysenburg.